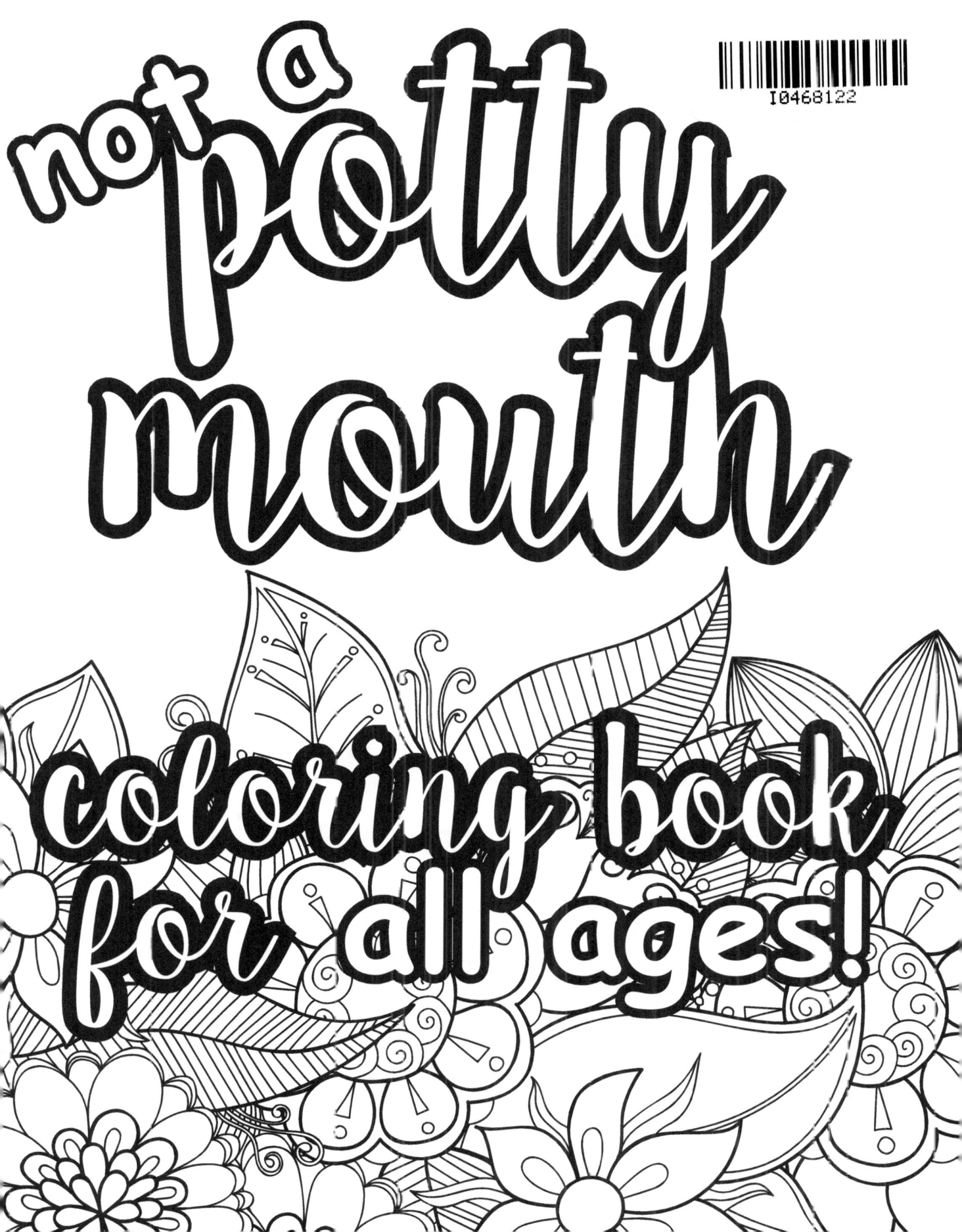

not a potty mouth

coloring book for all ages!

I0468122

Non-Potty Mouth
Coloring Book for Kids

Copyright © 2016 by JA Hildreth

Cover by: Creative Book Concepts

ISBN-13: 978-1530867691

Printed in U.S.A

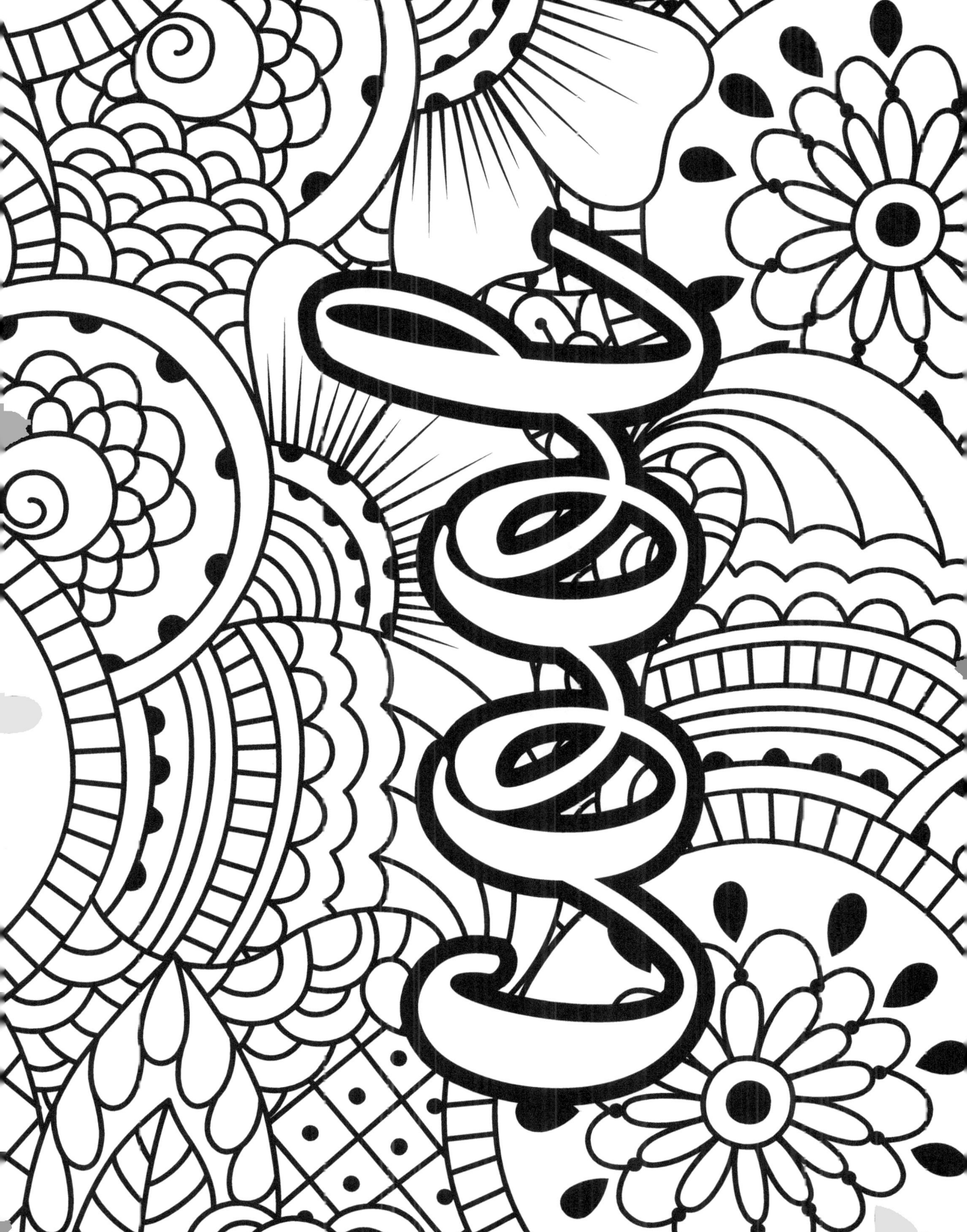

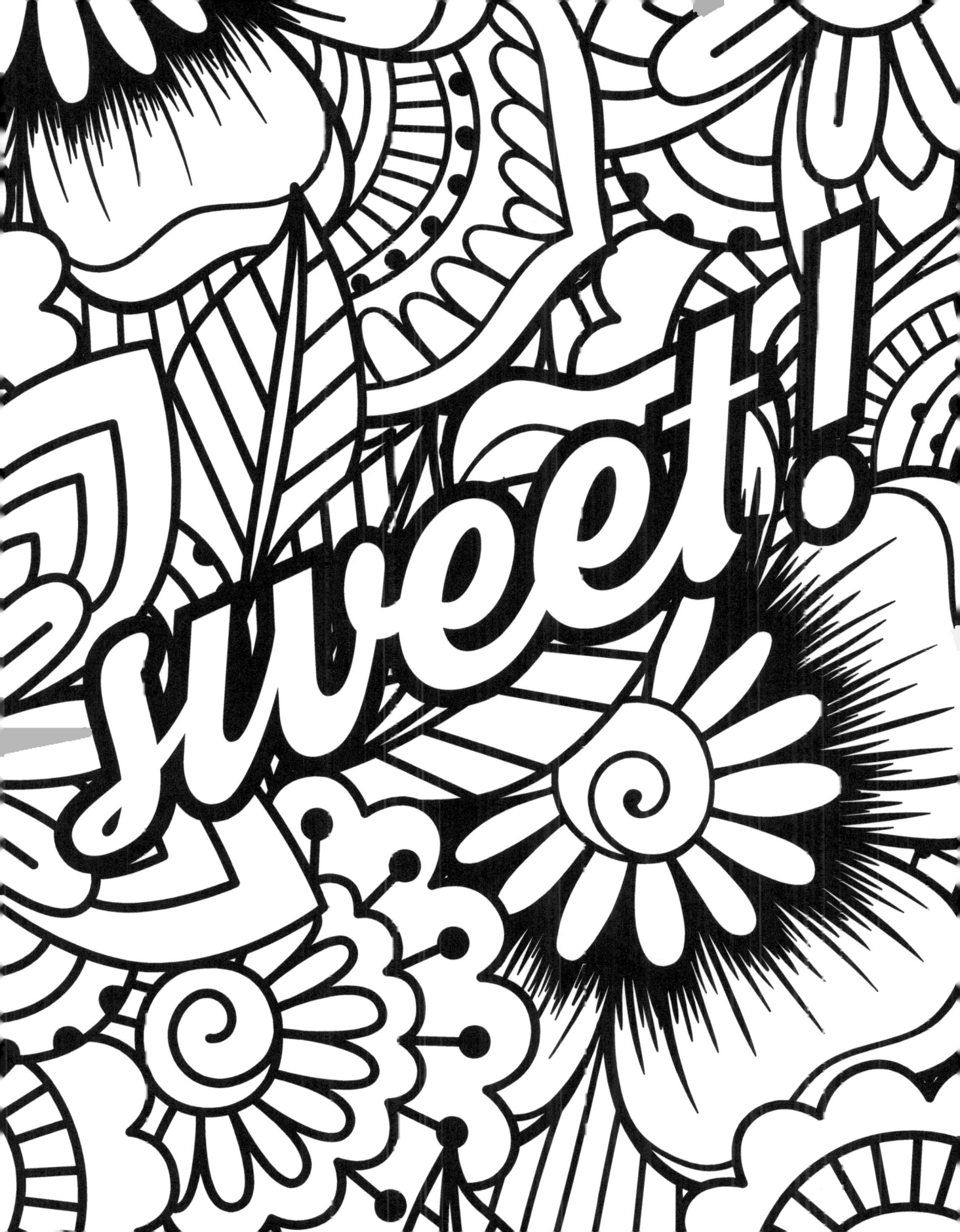

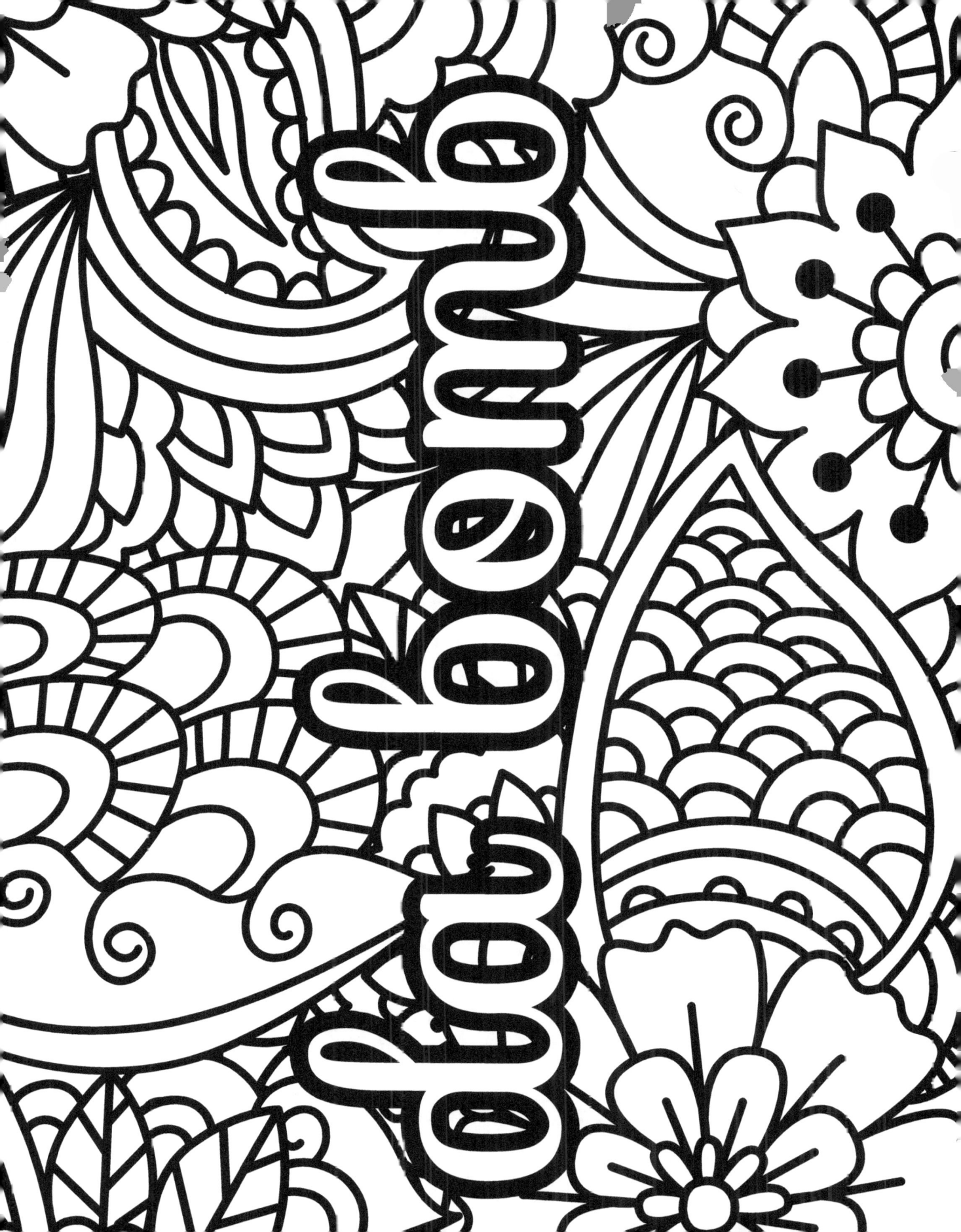

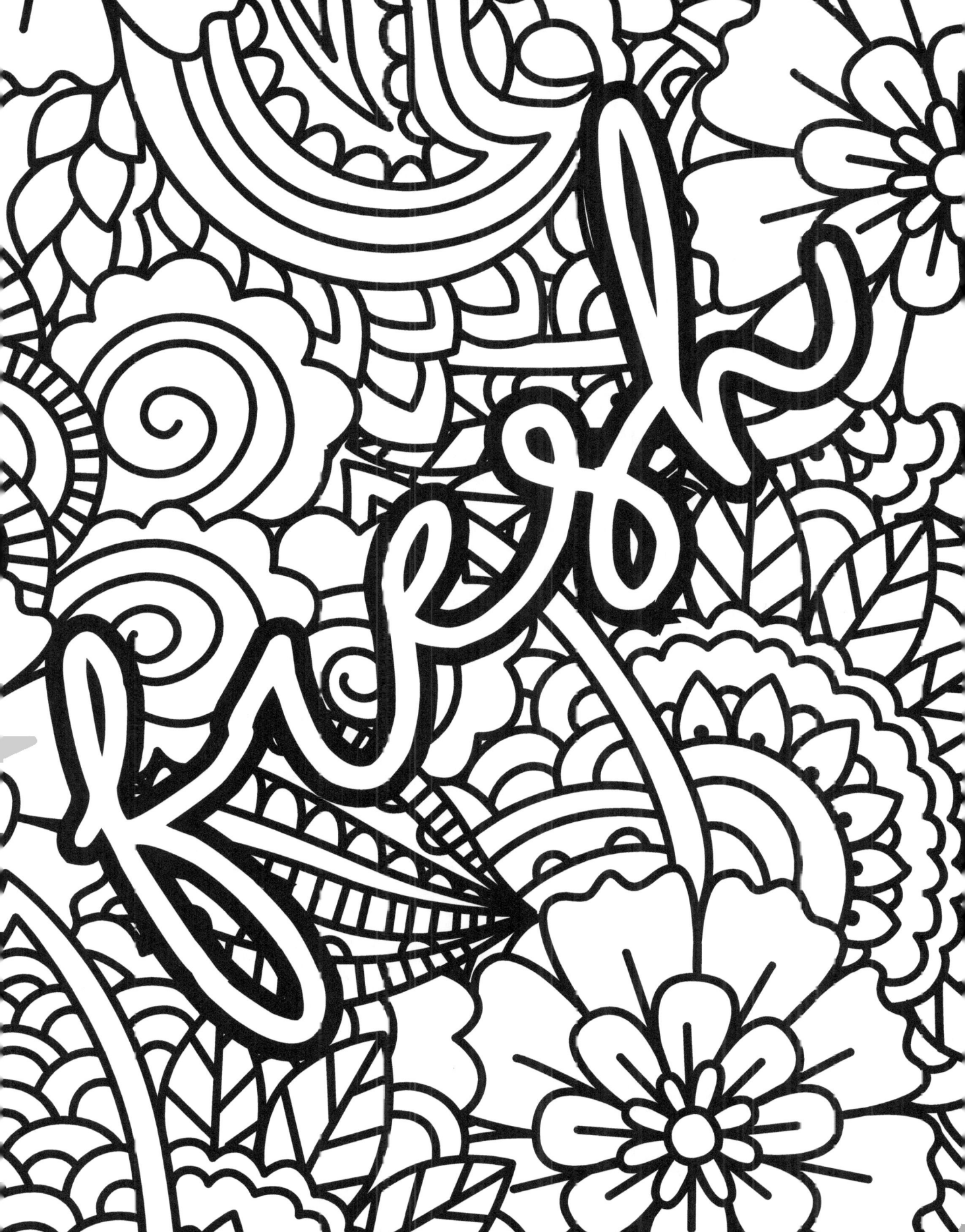

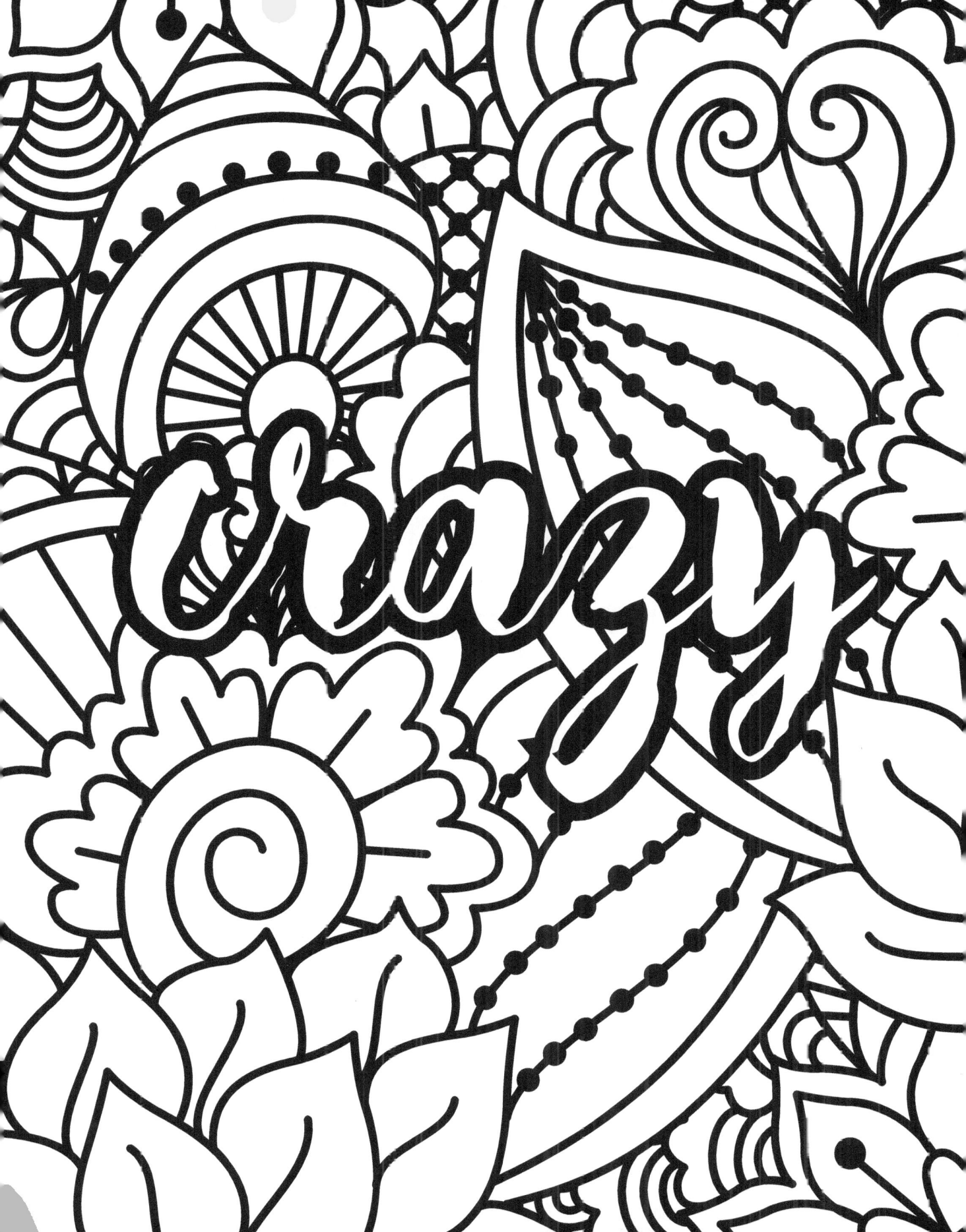

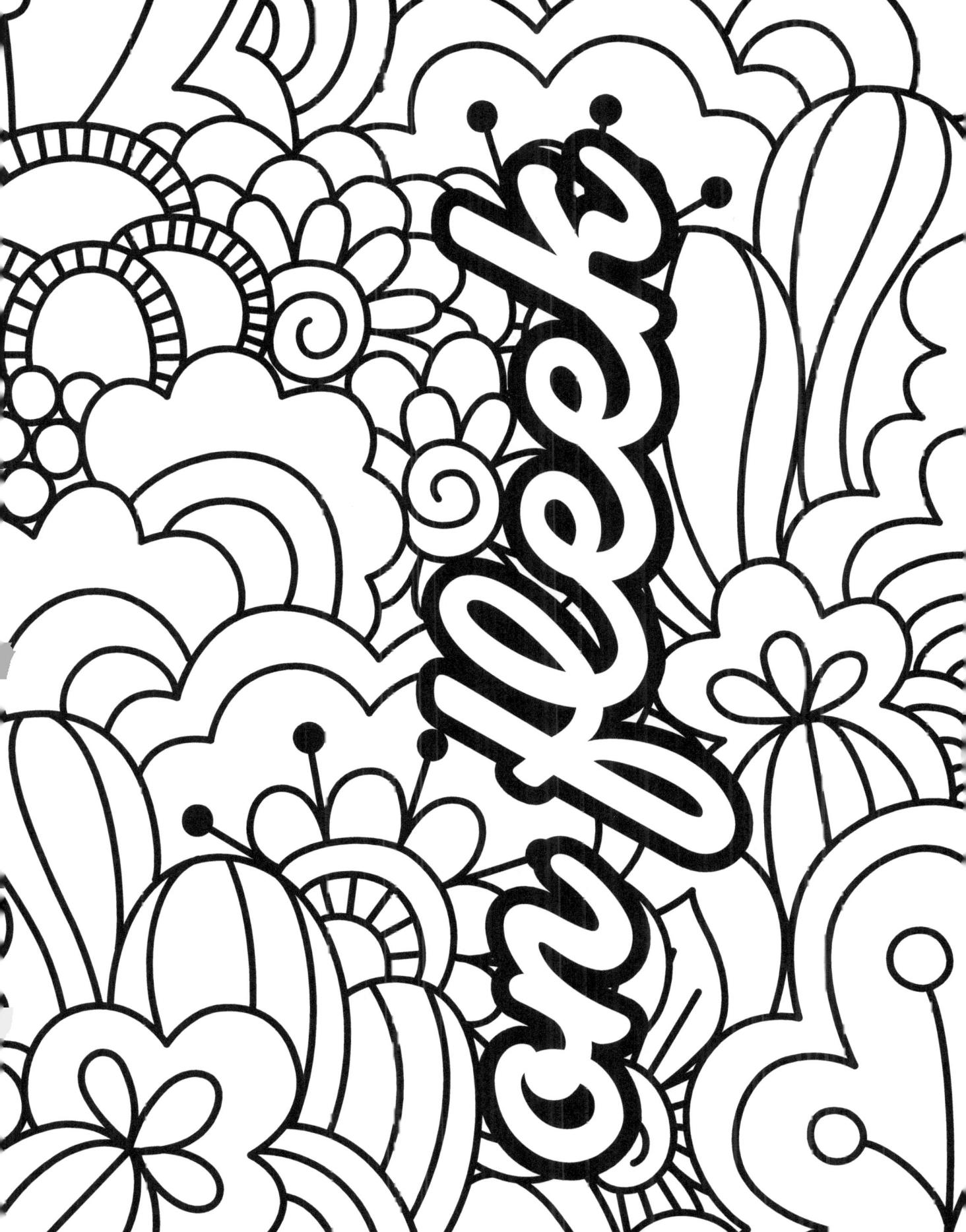

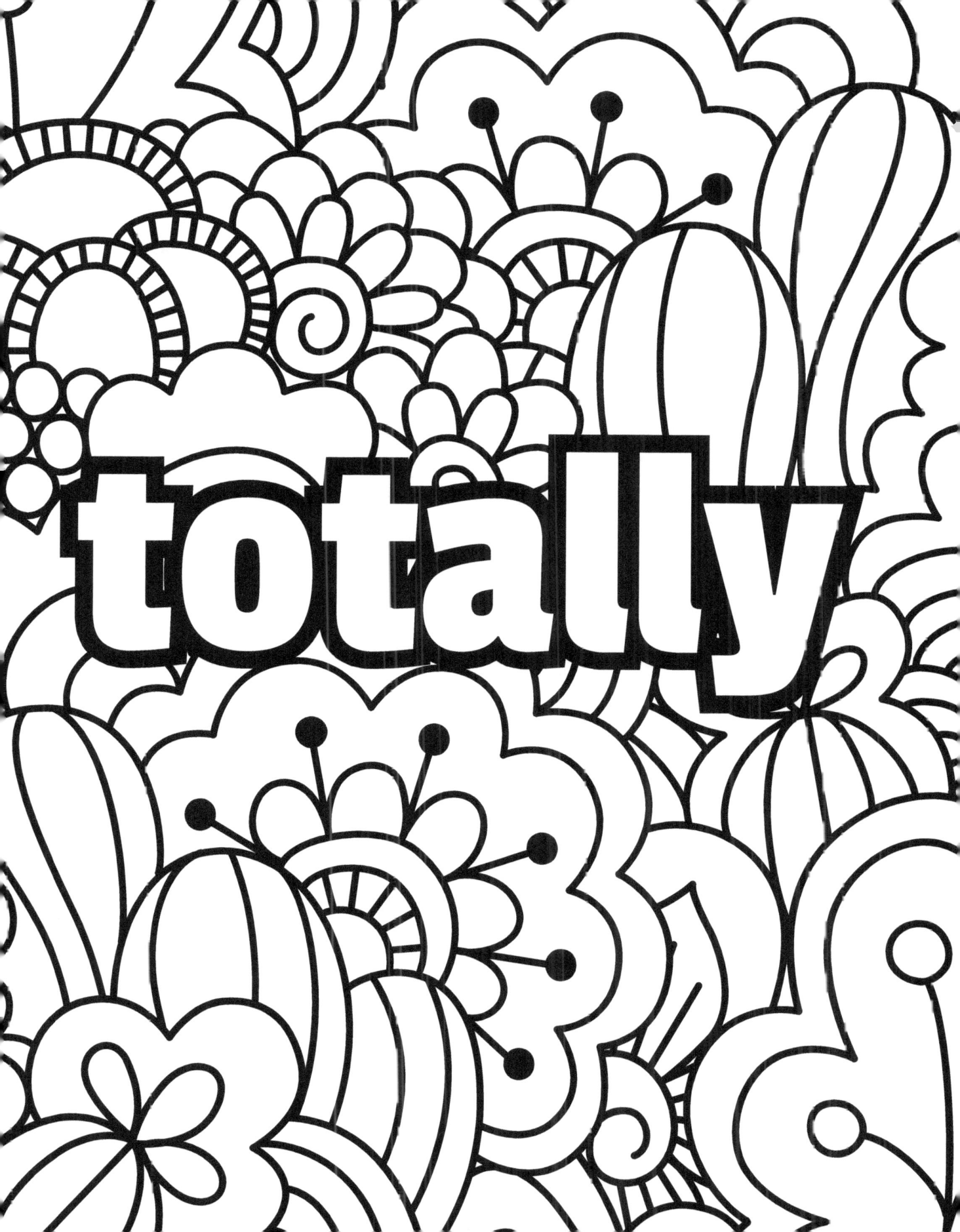

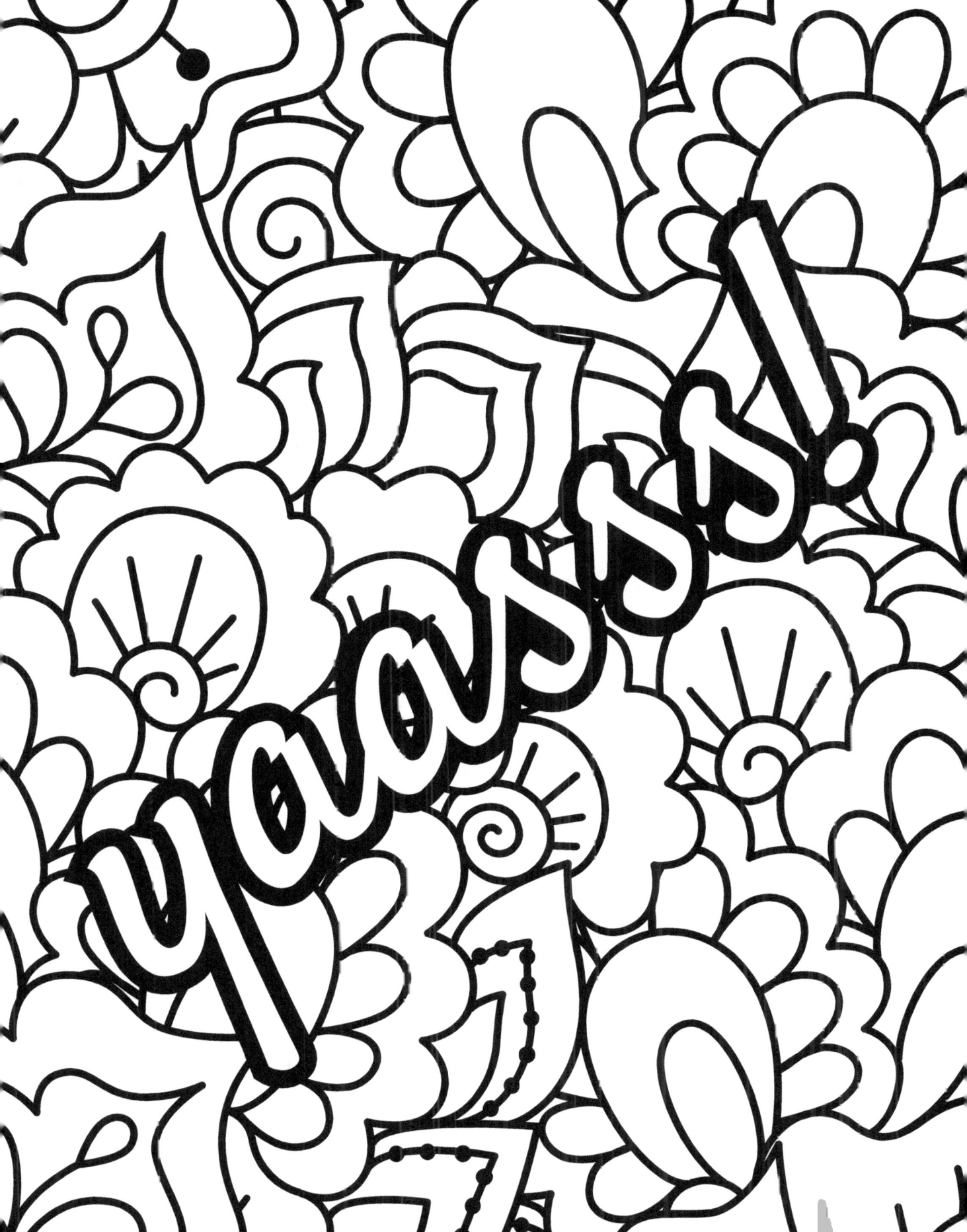

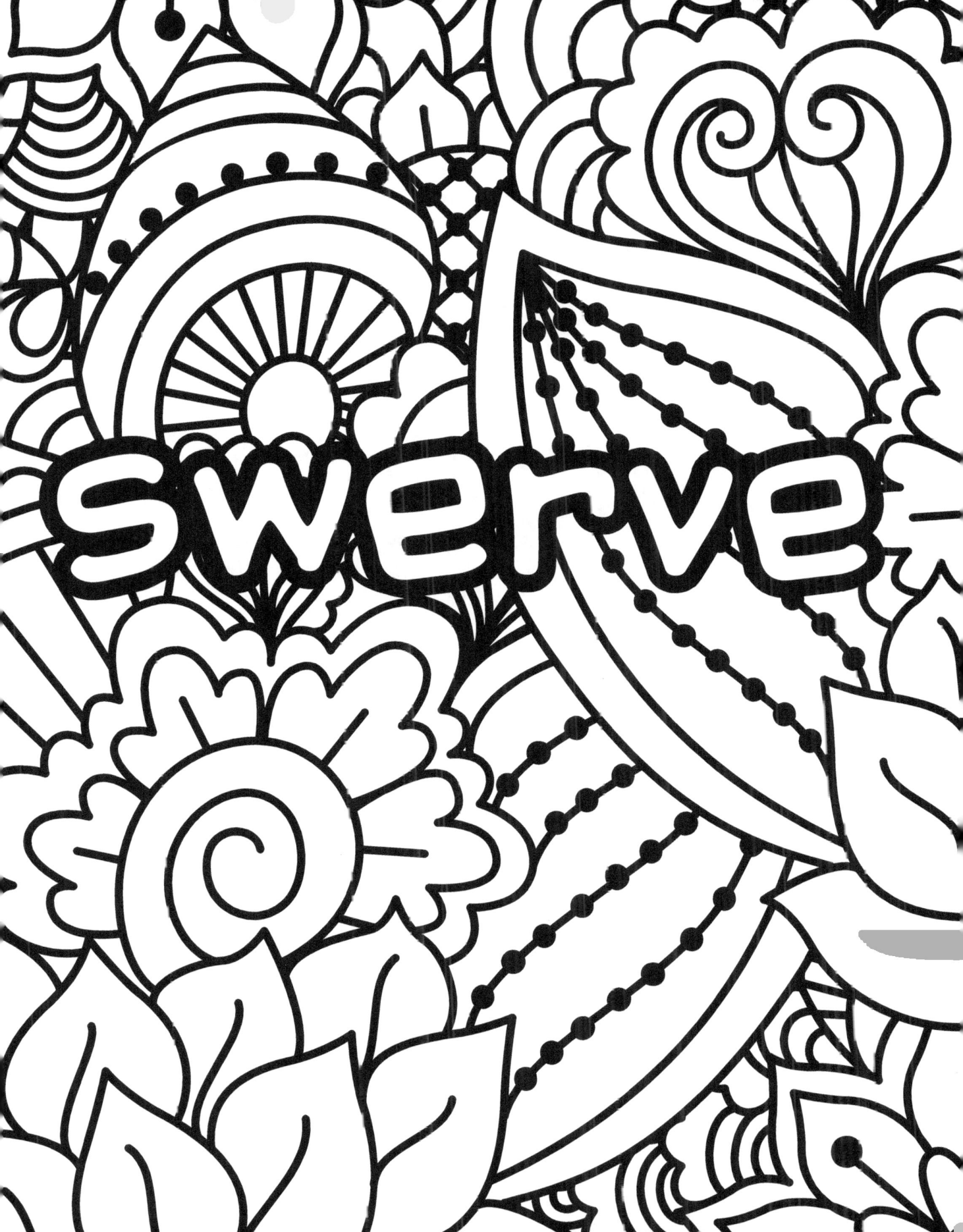

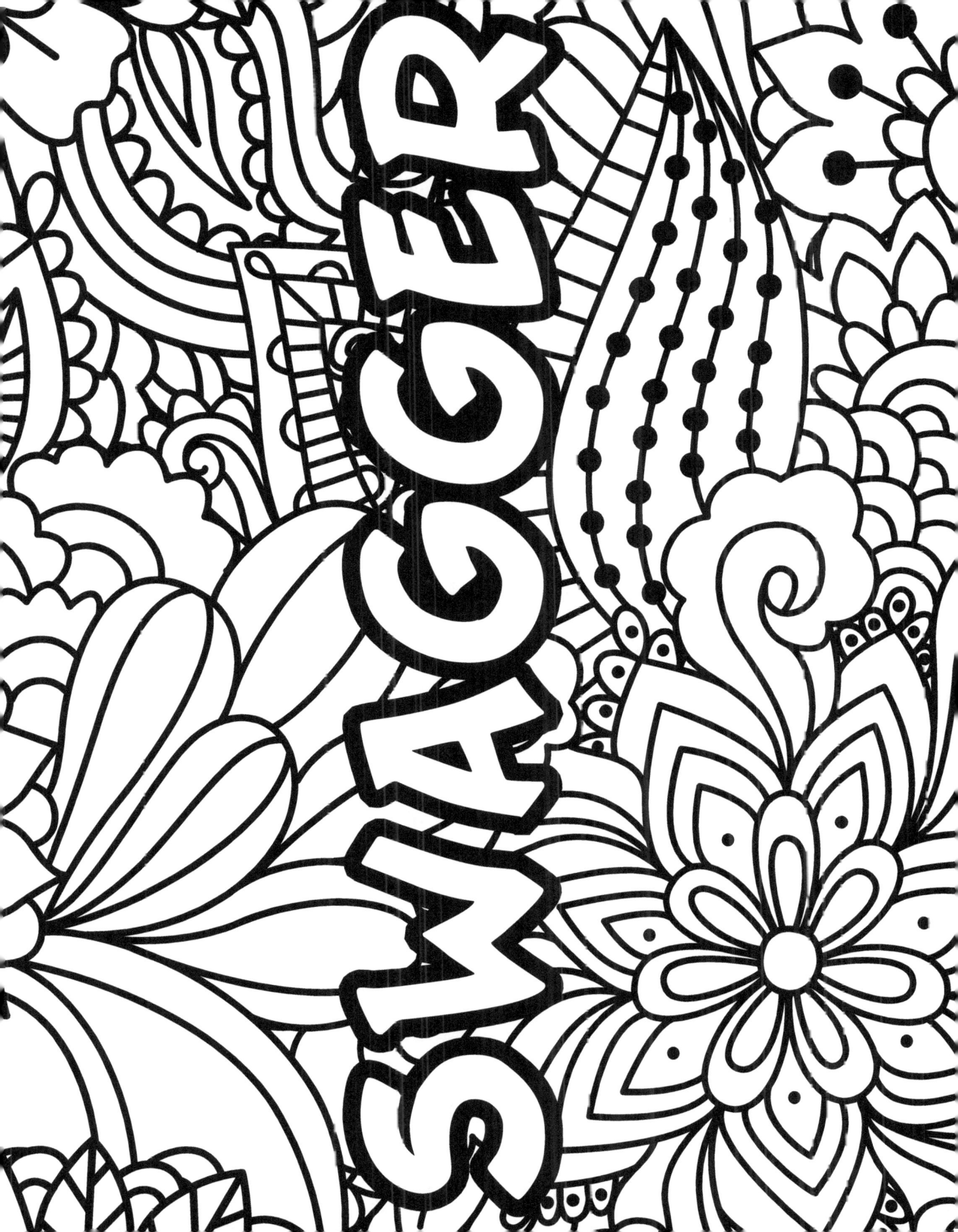

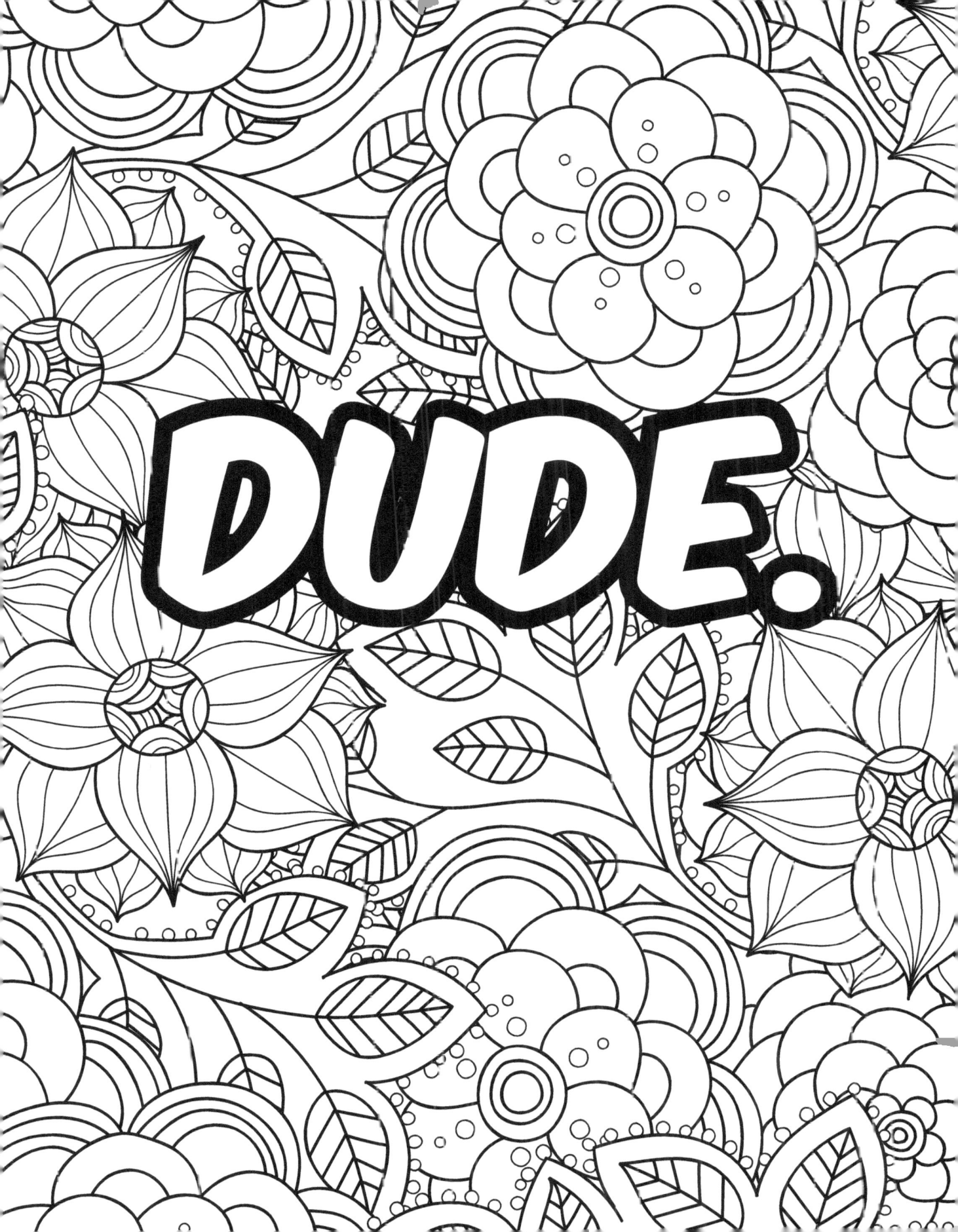

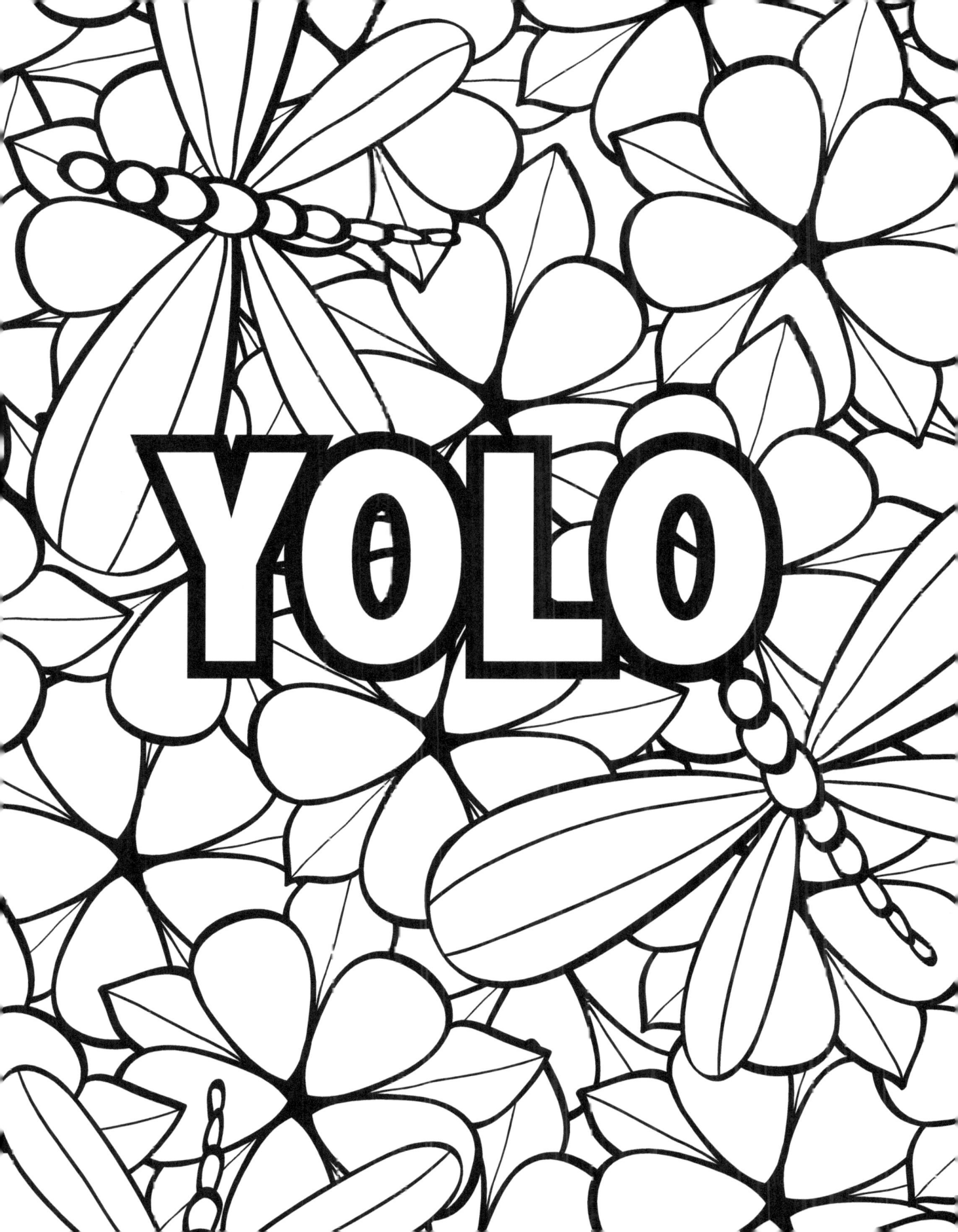

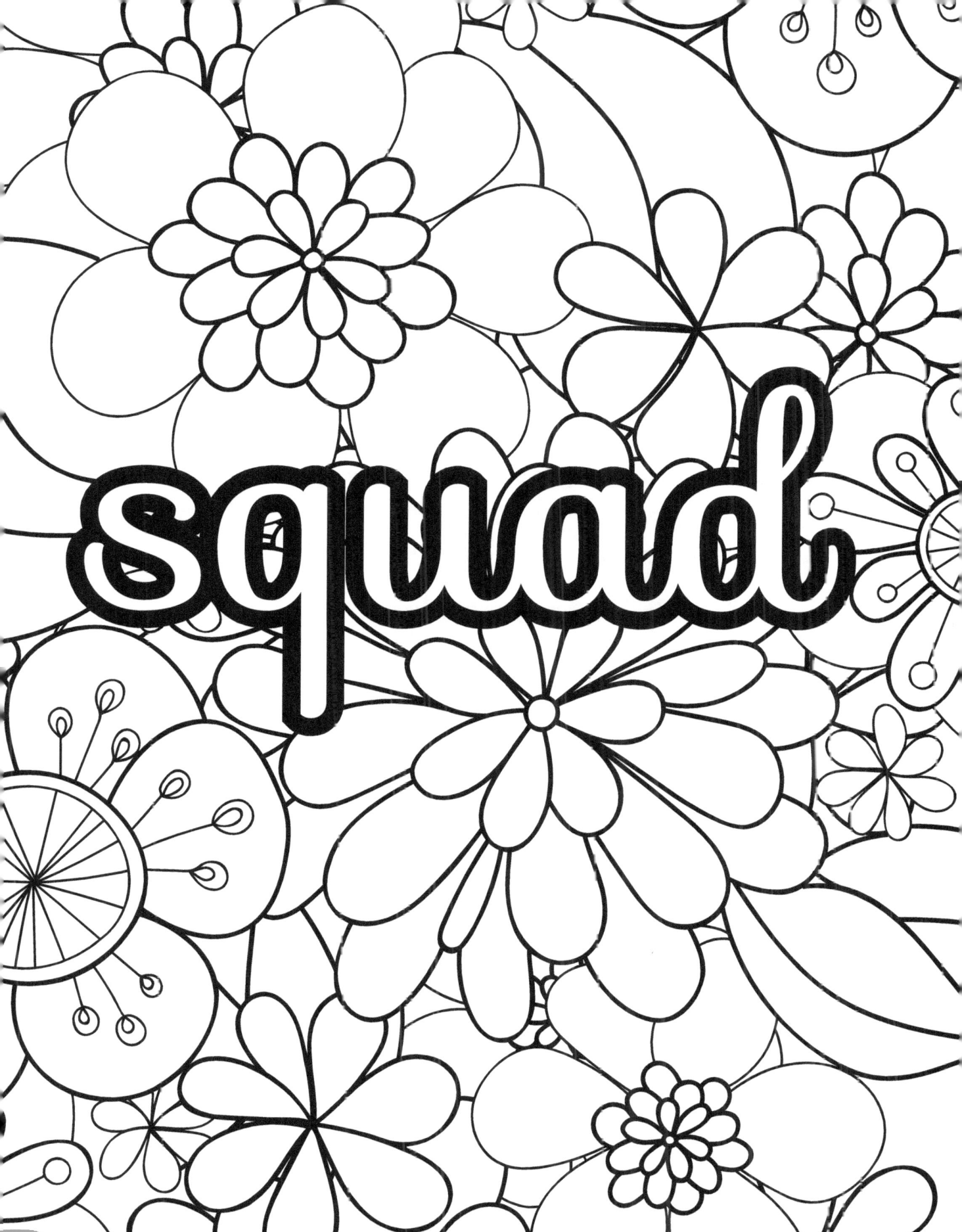

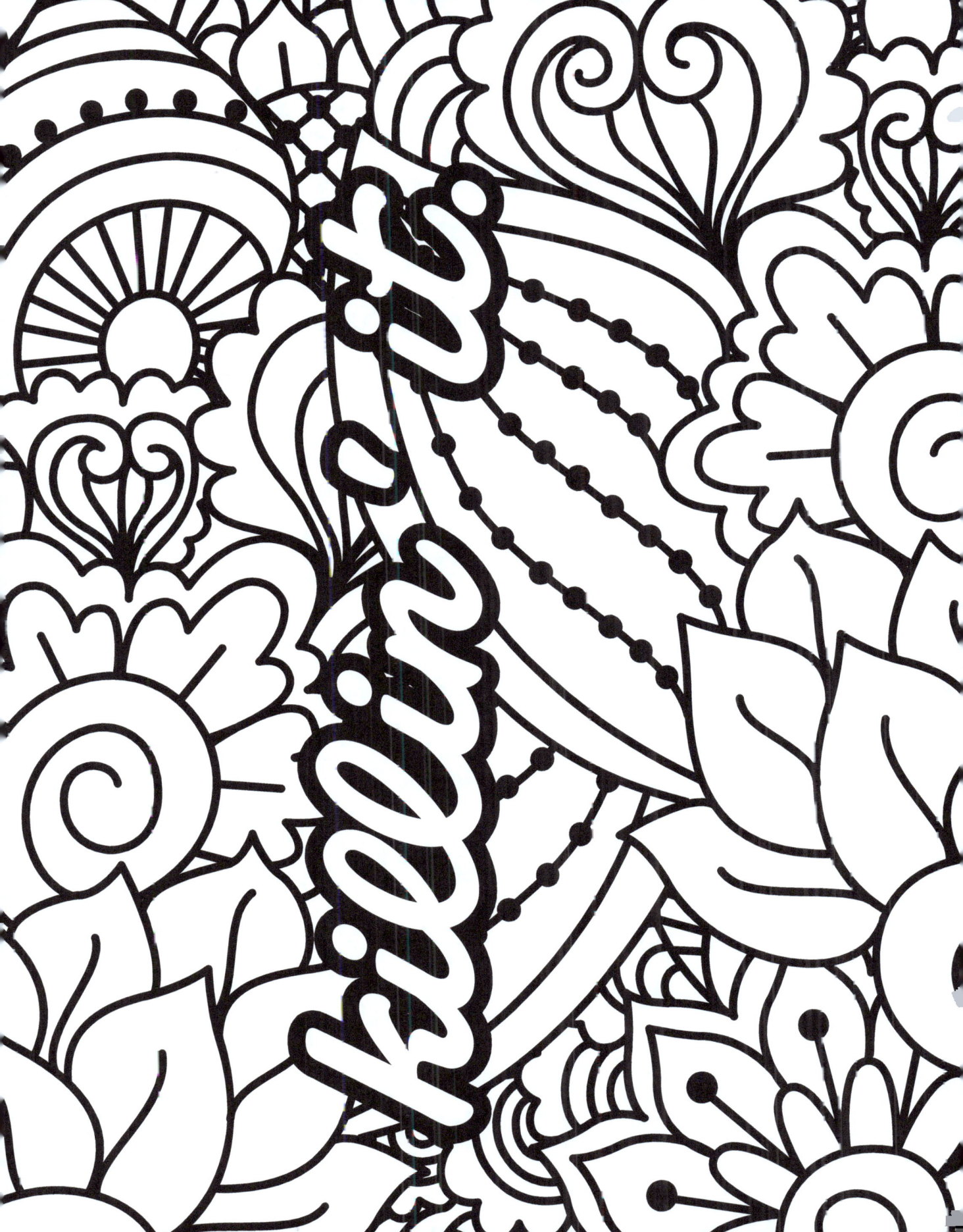

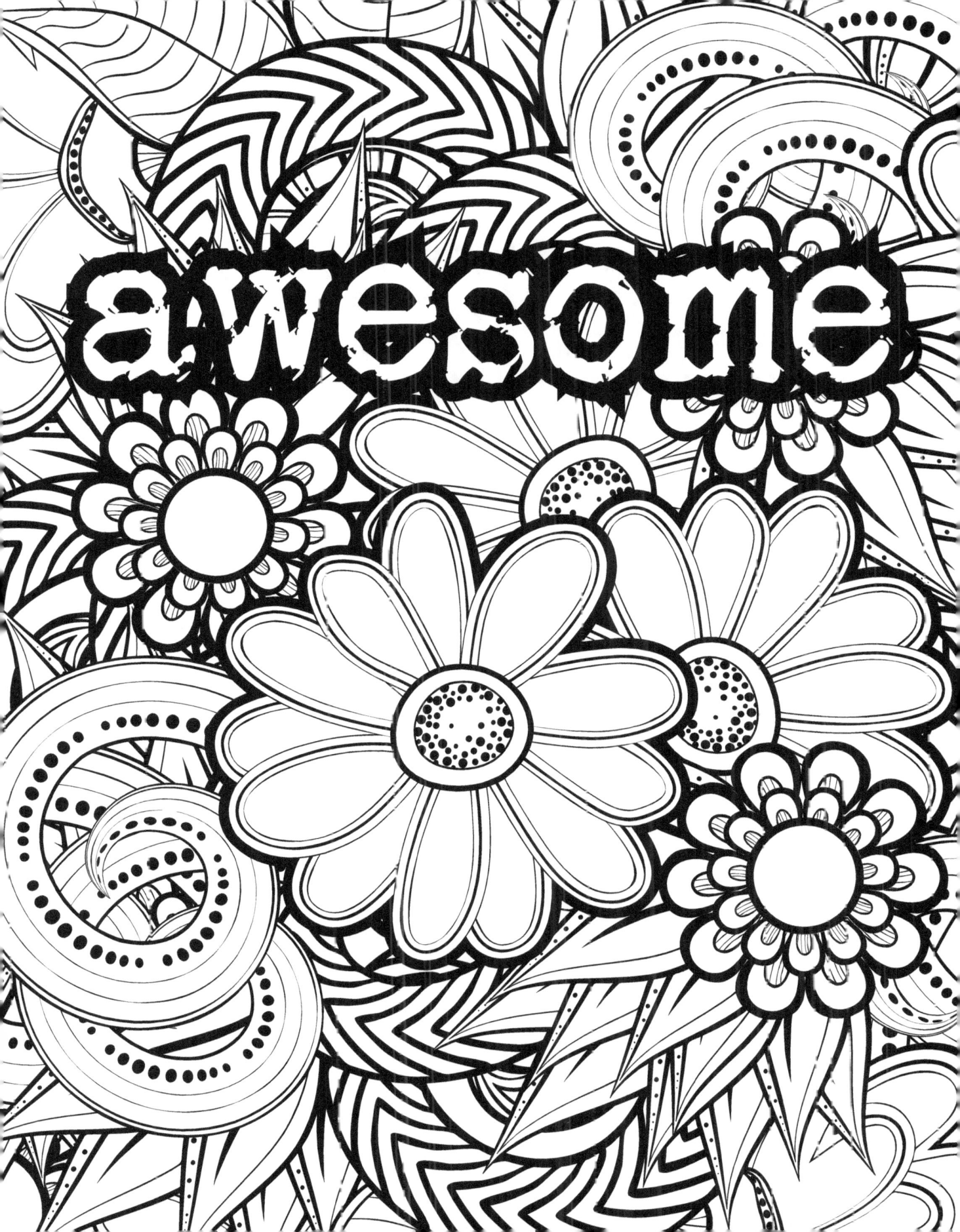

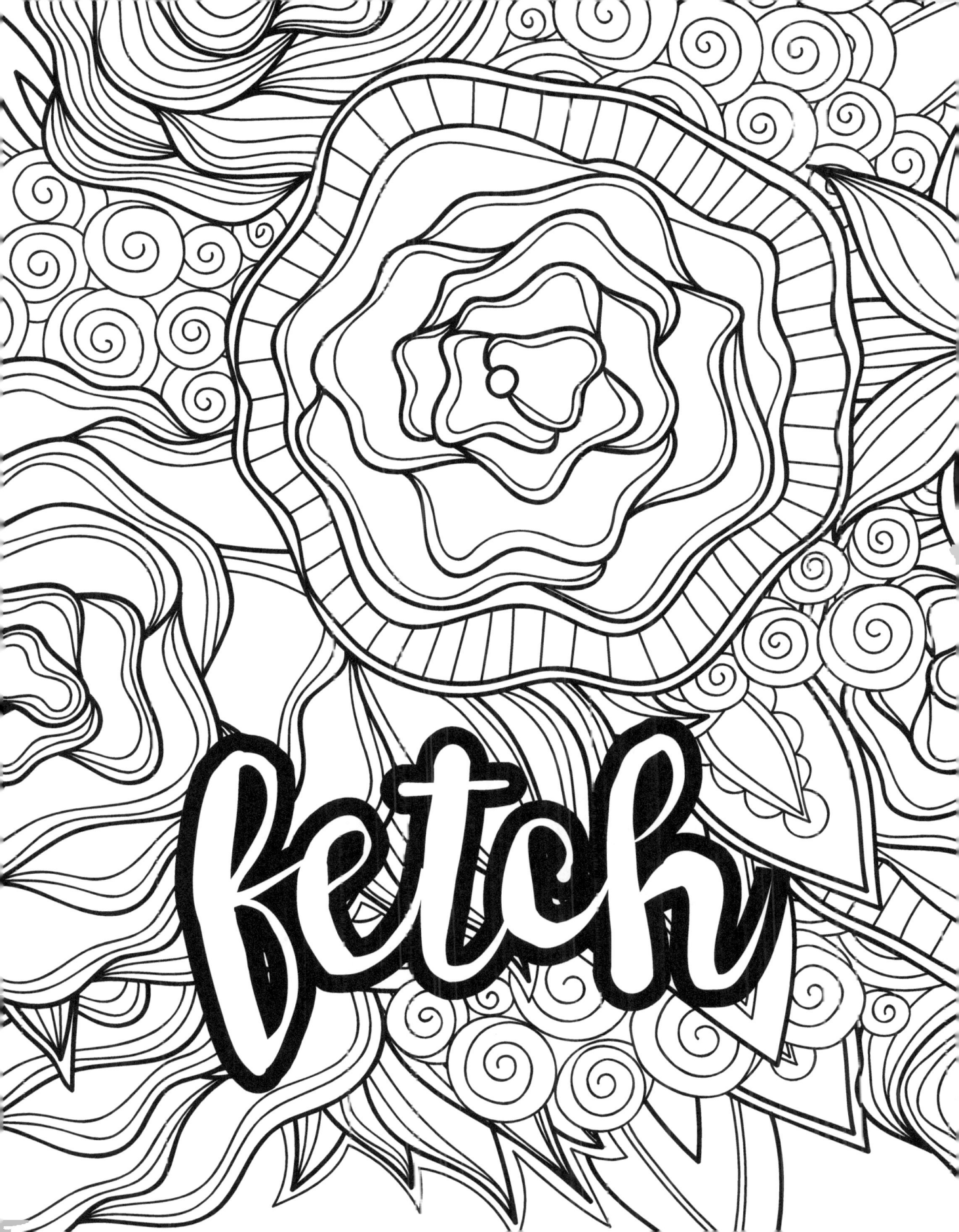

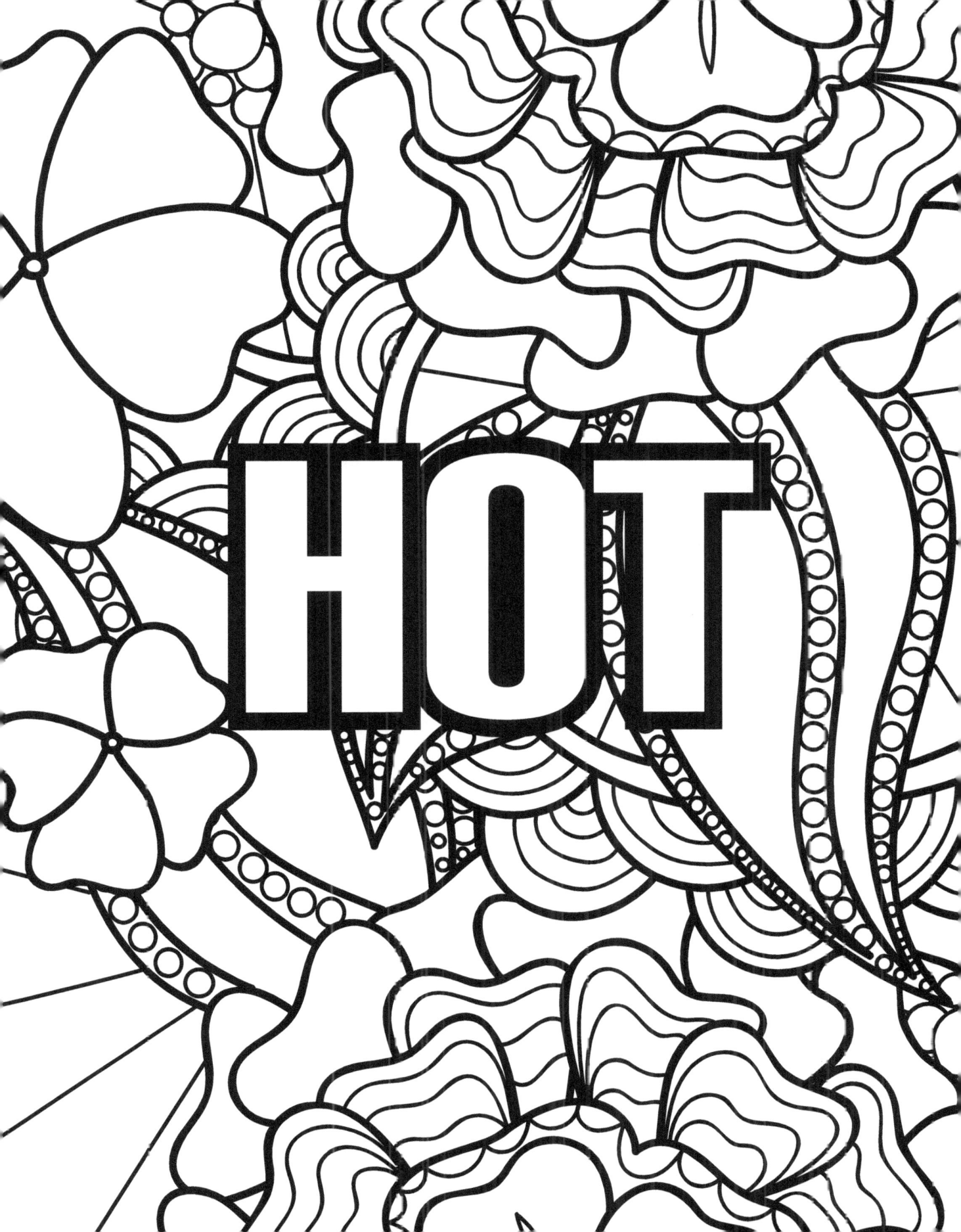

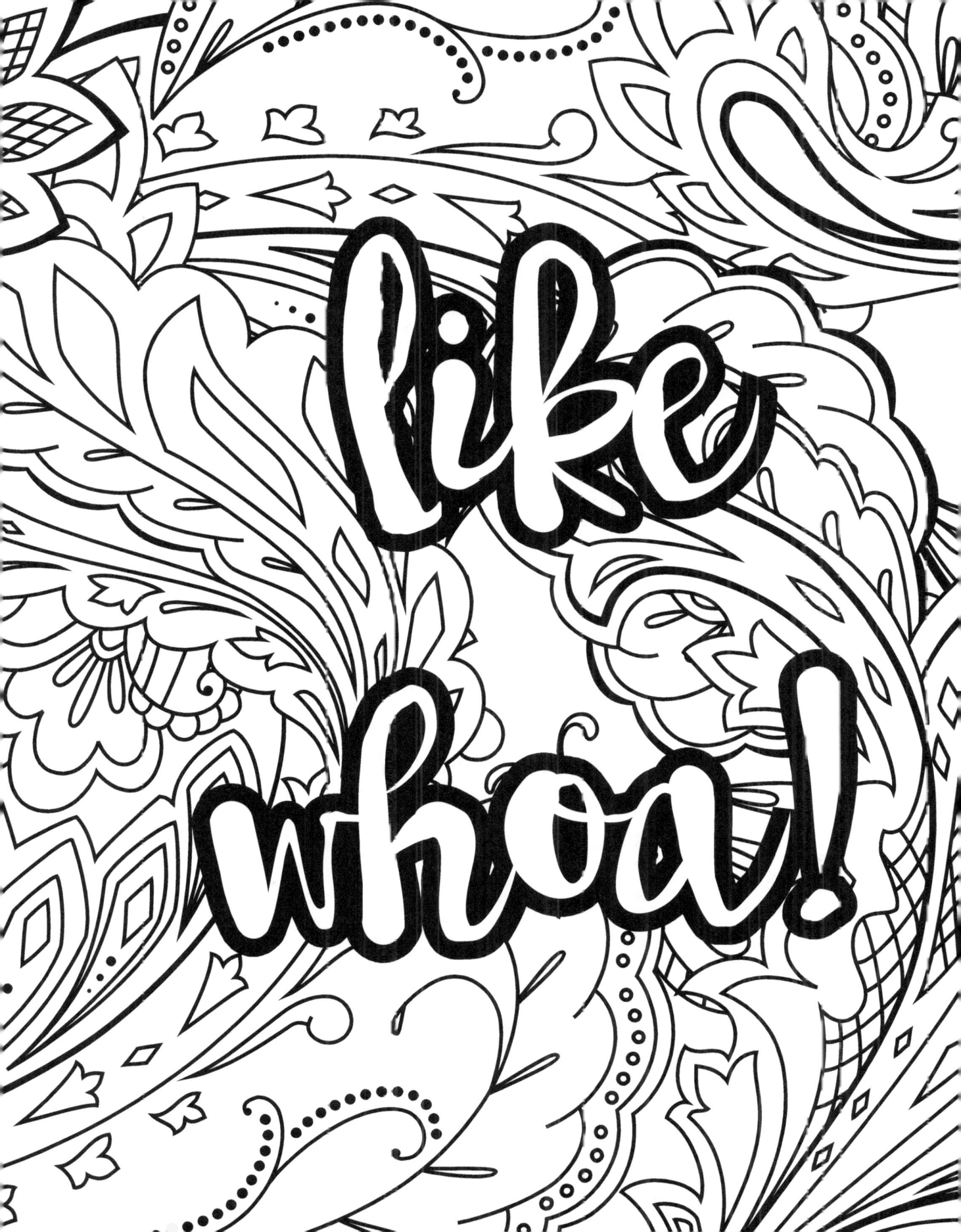

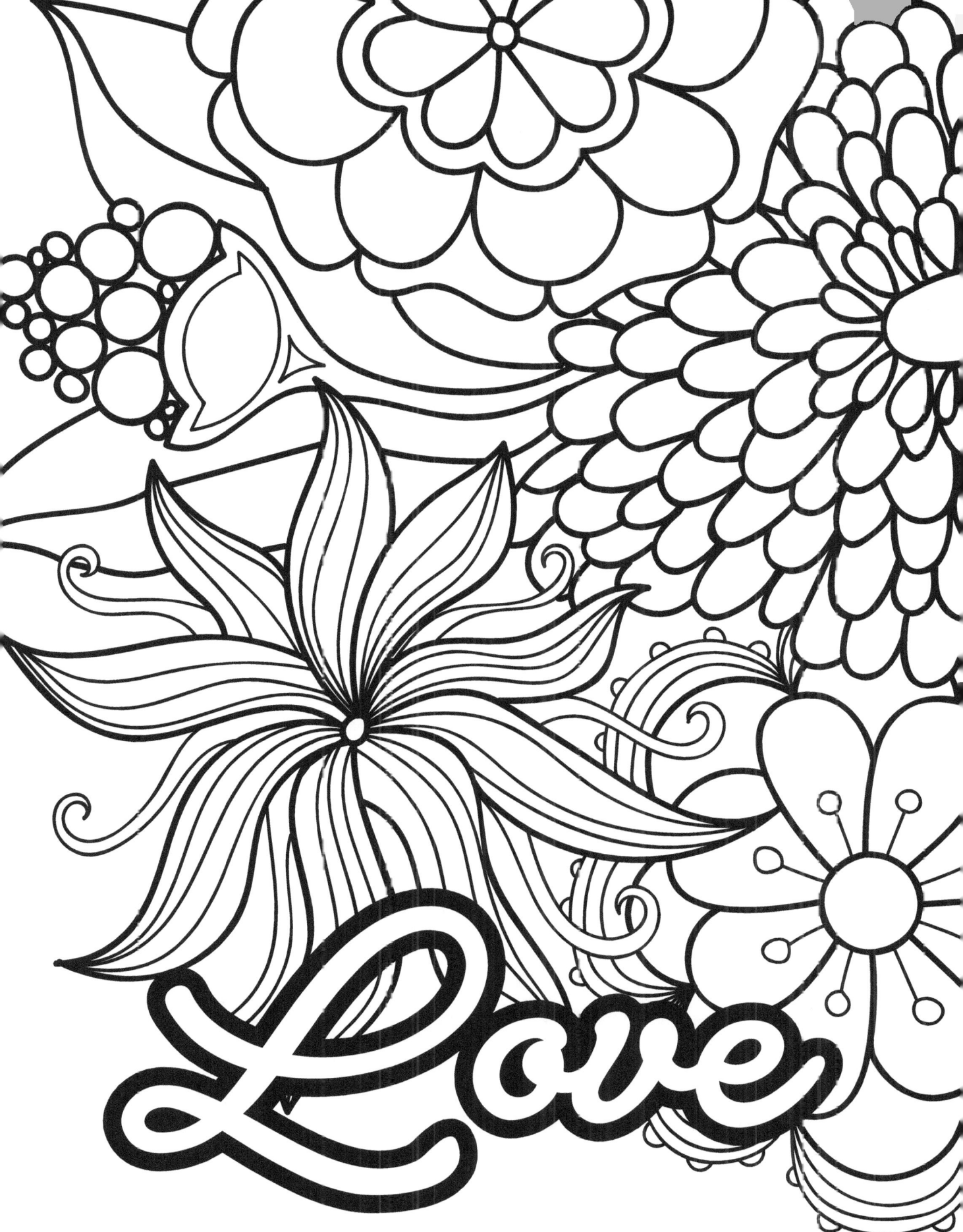

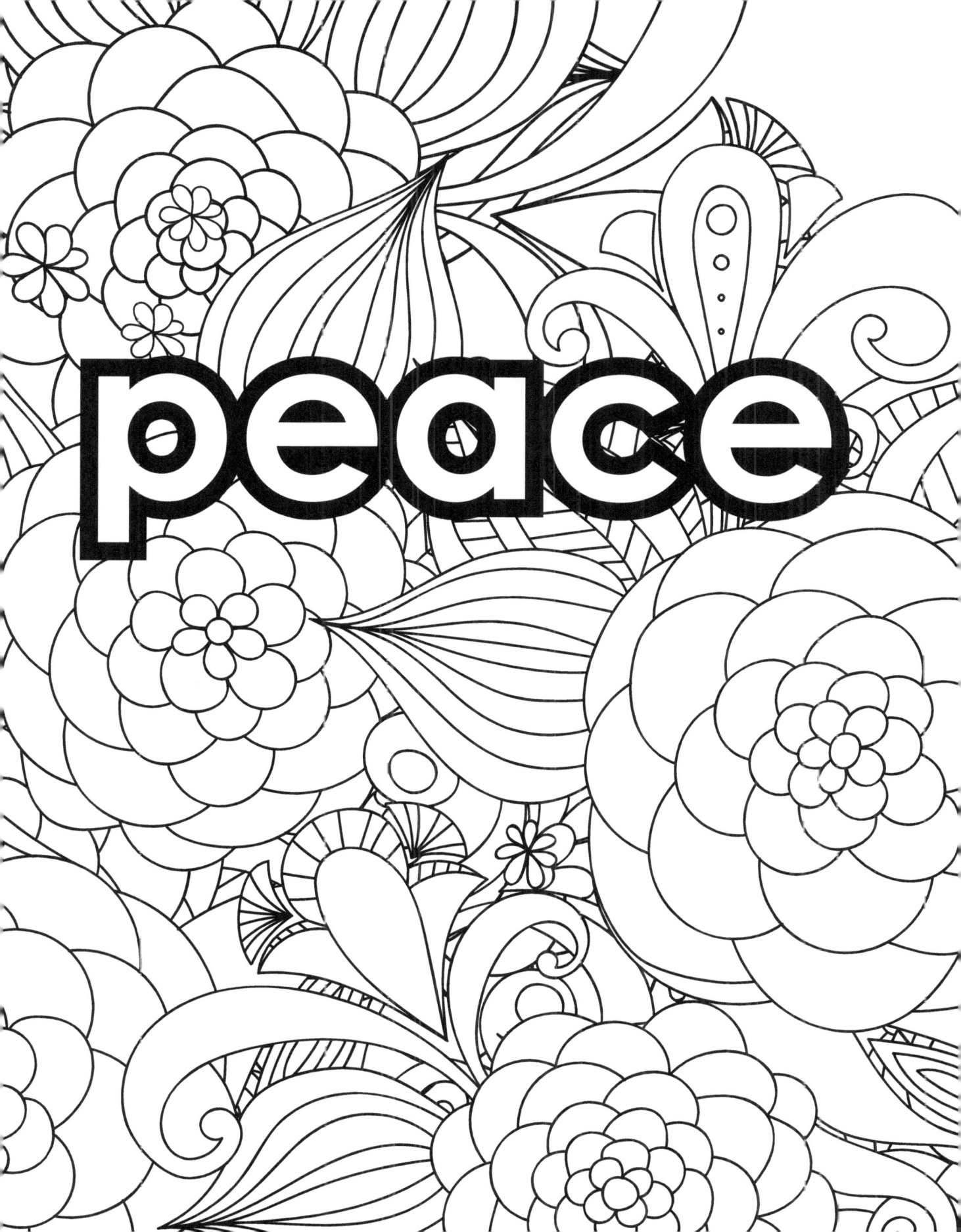

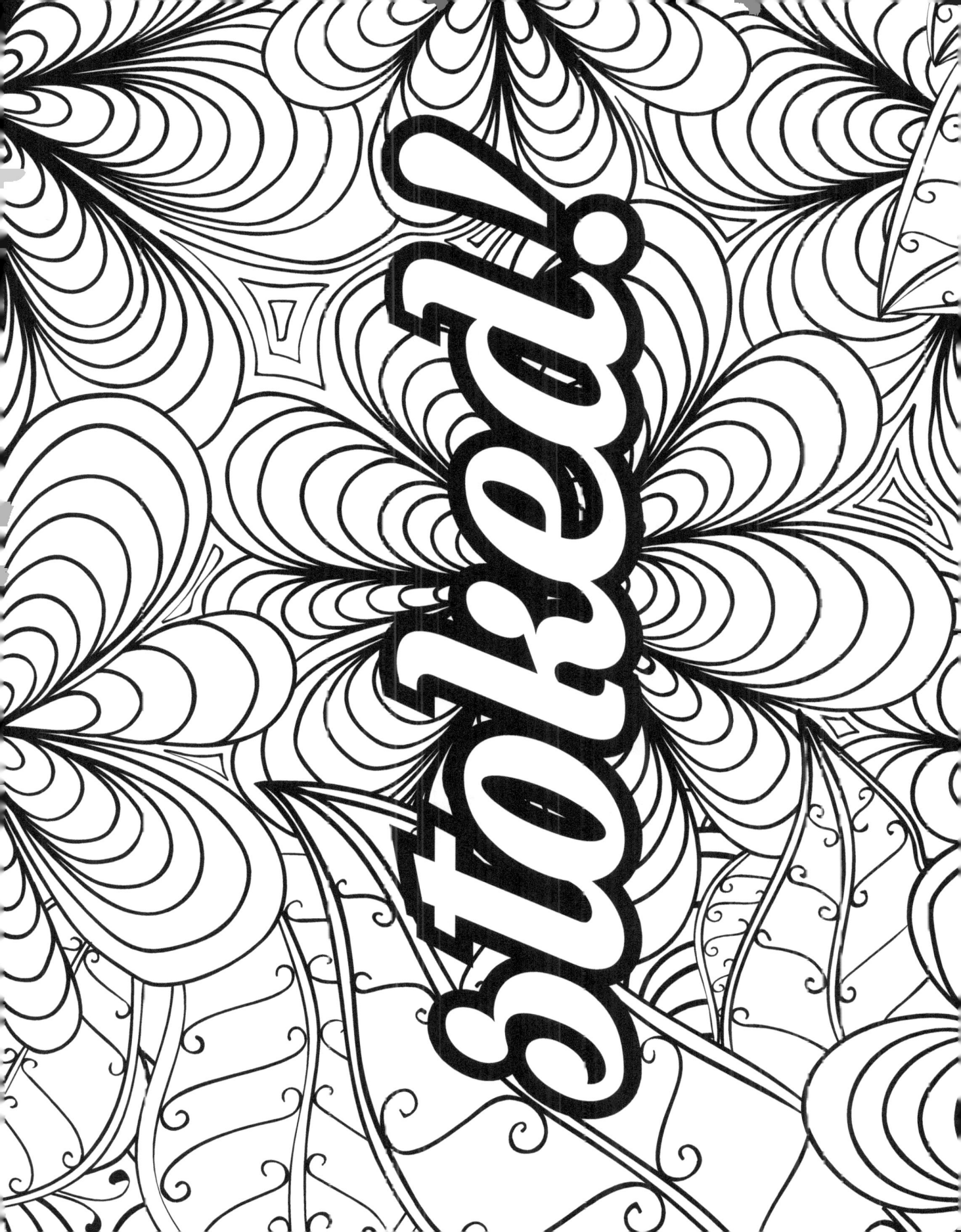

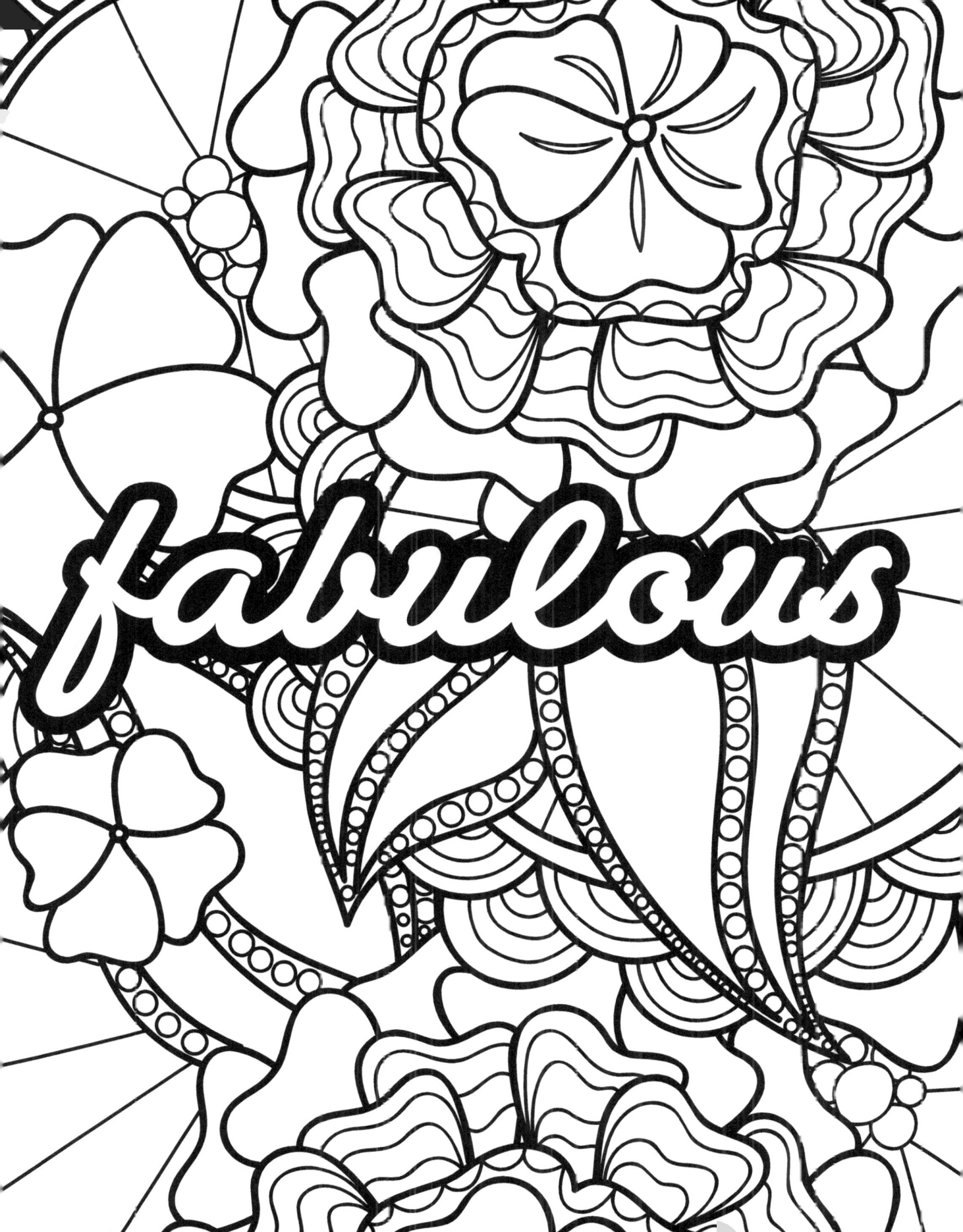

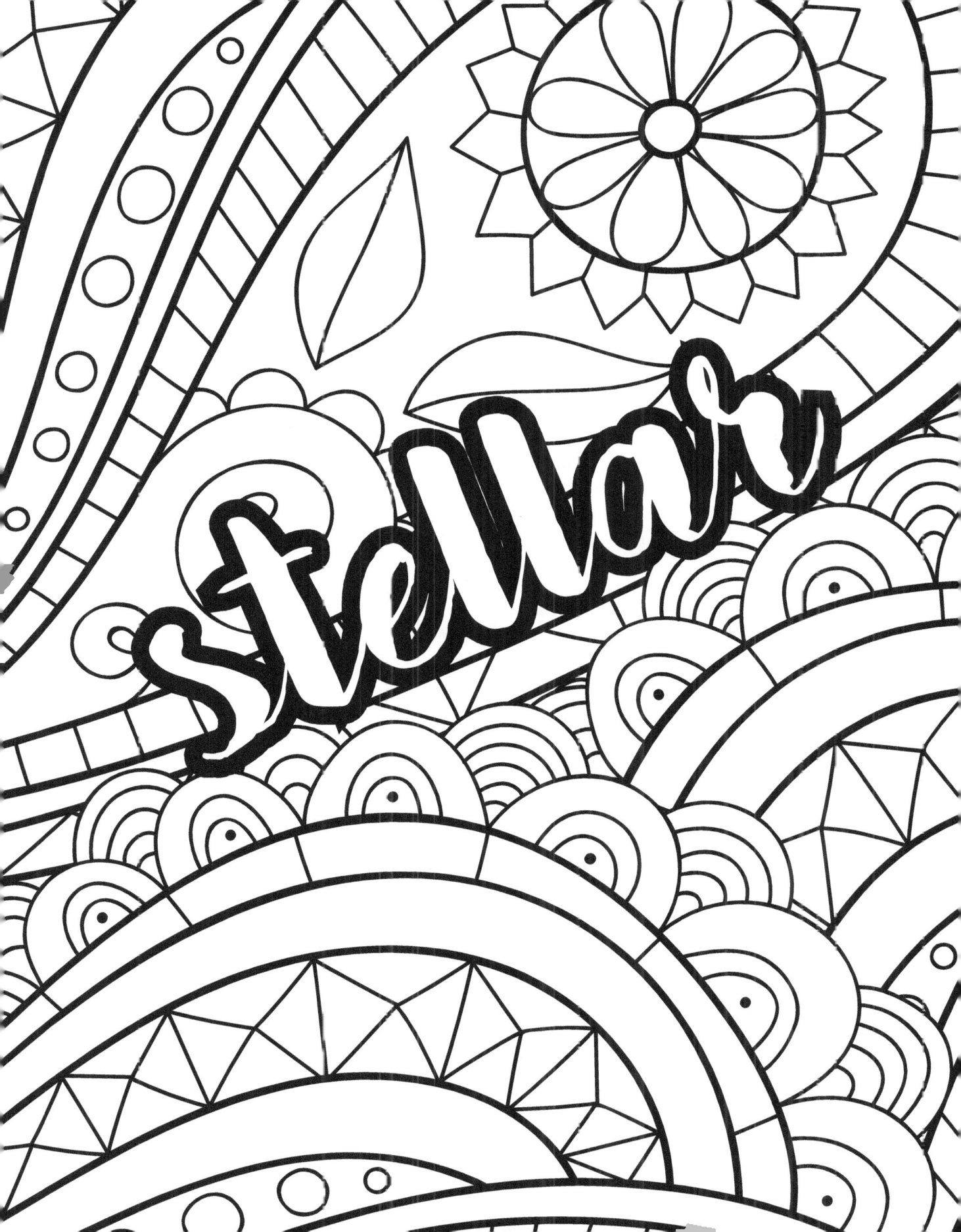

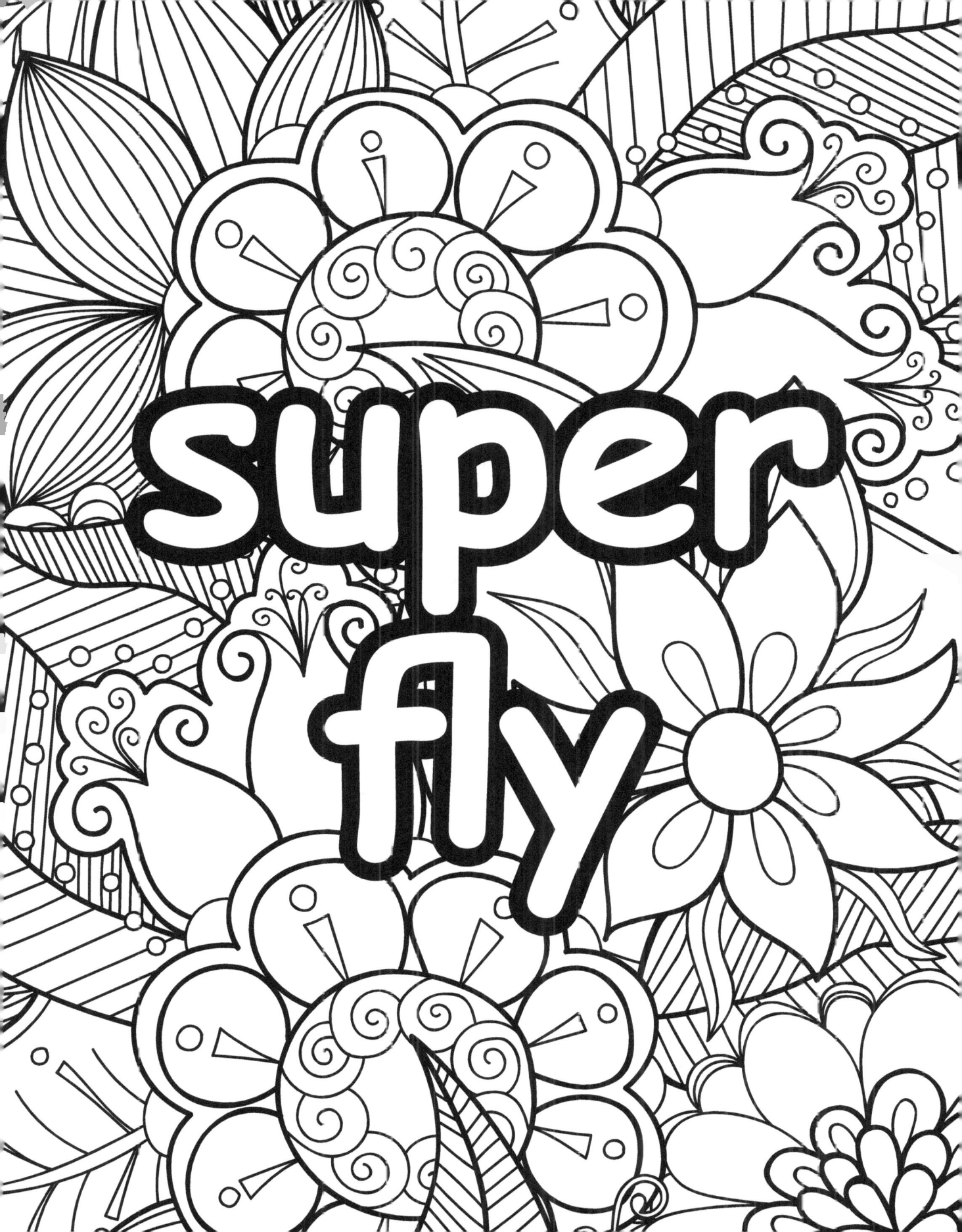

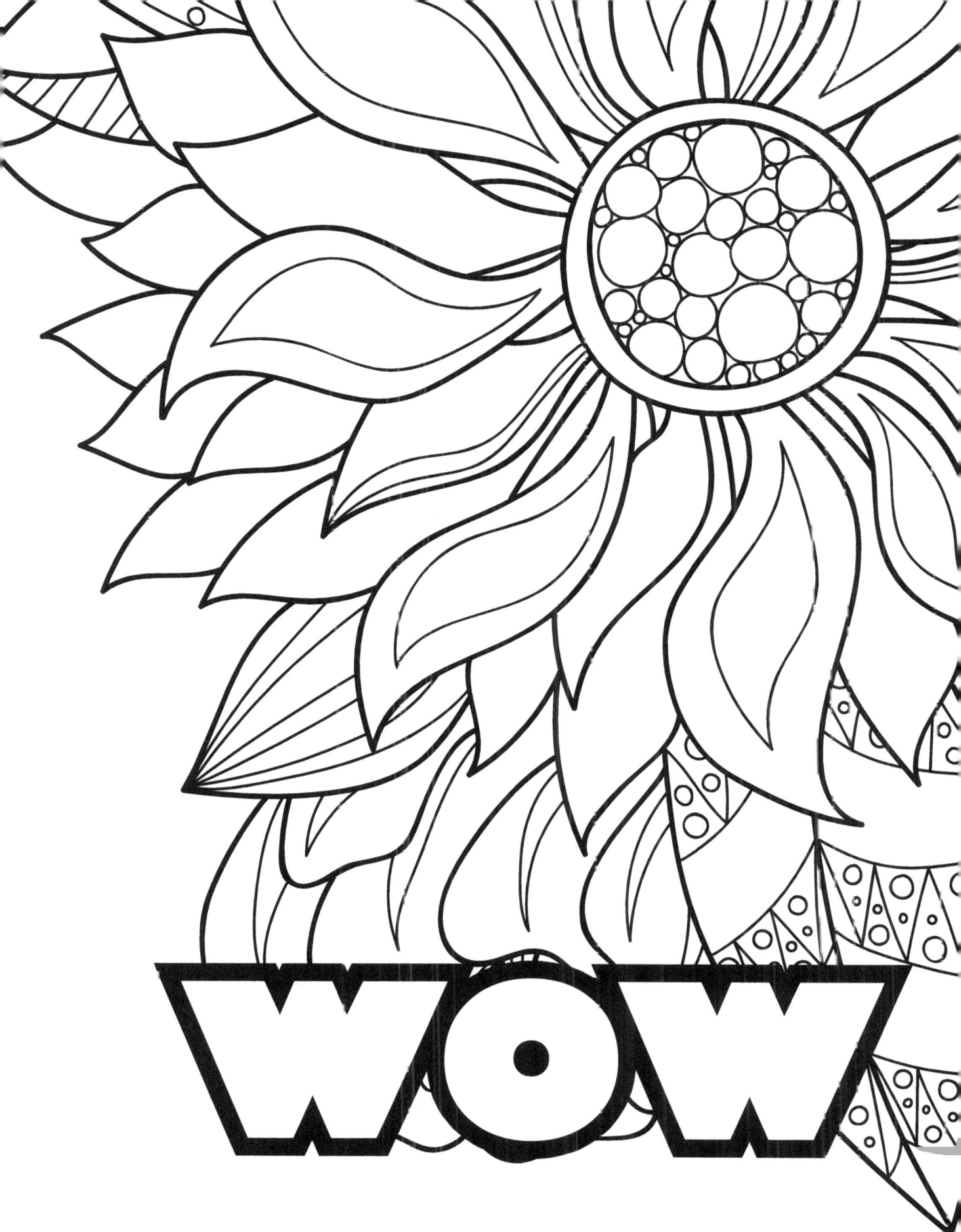

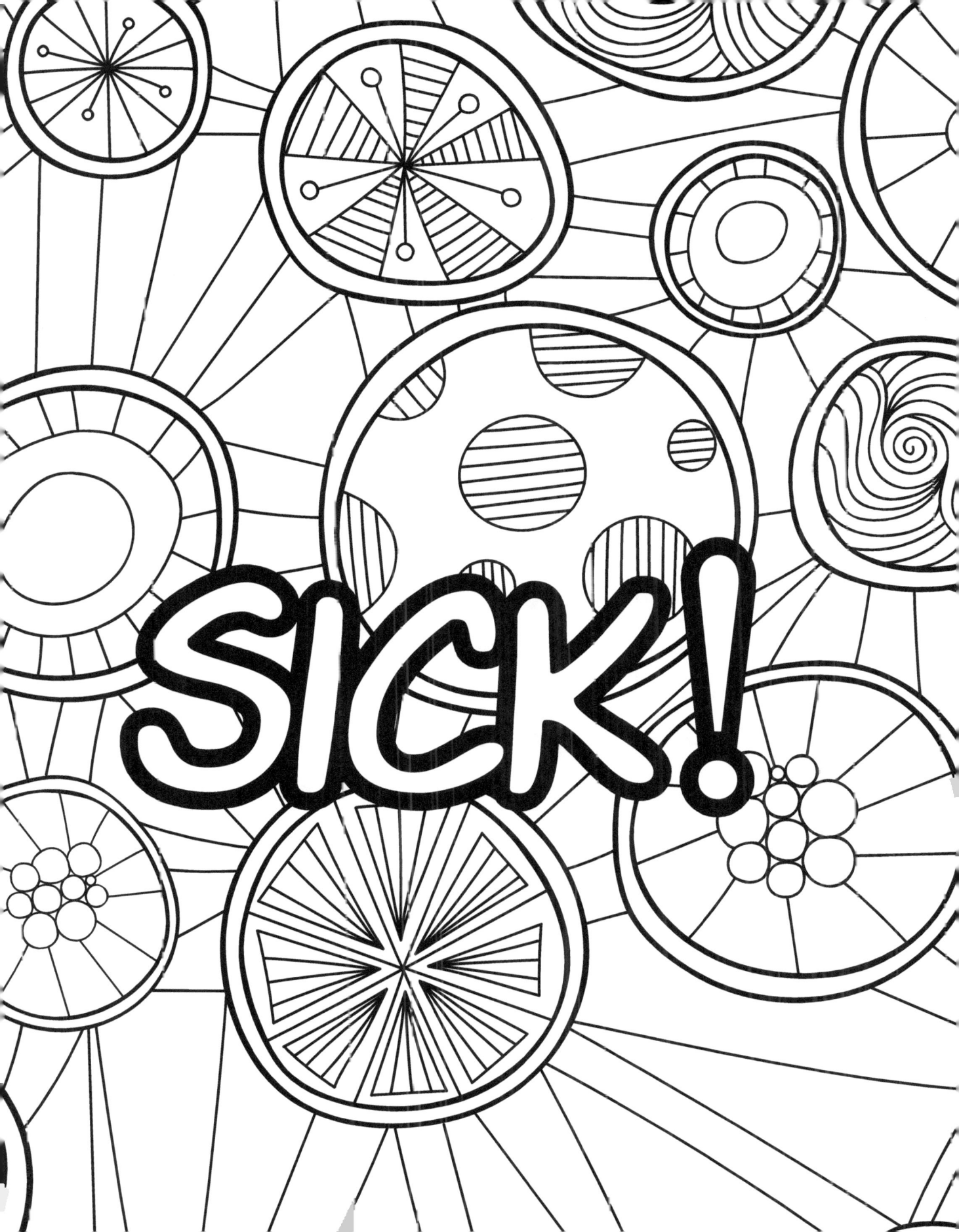

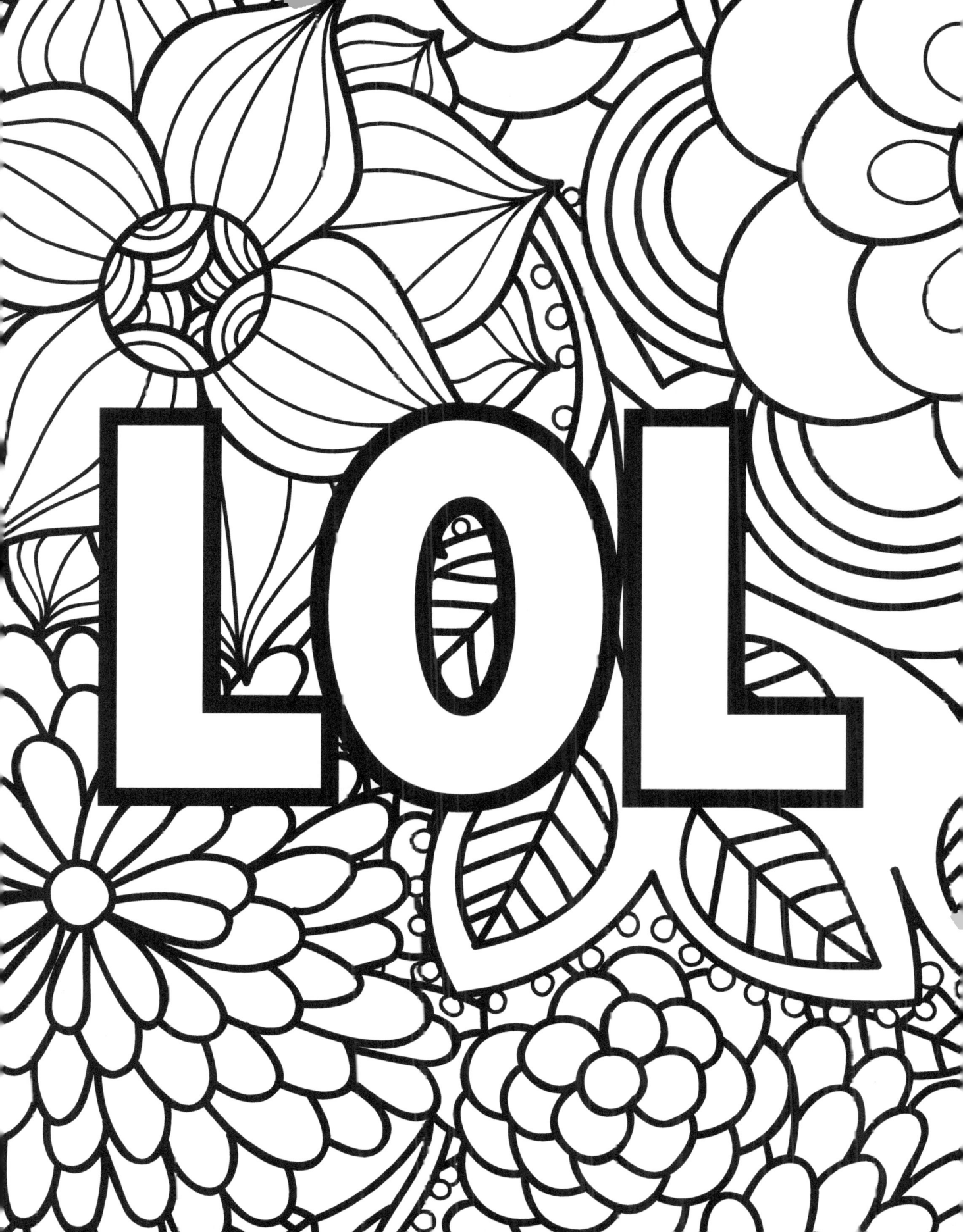

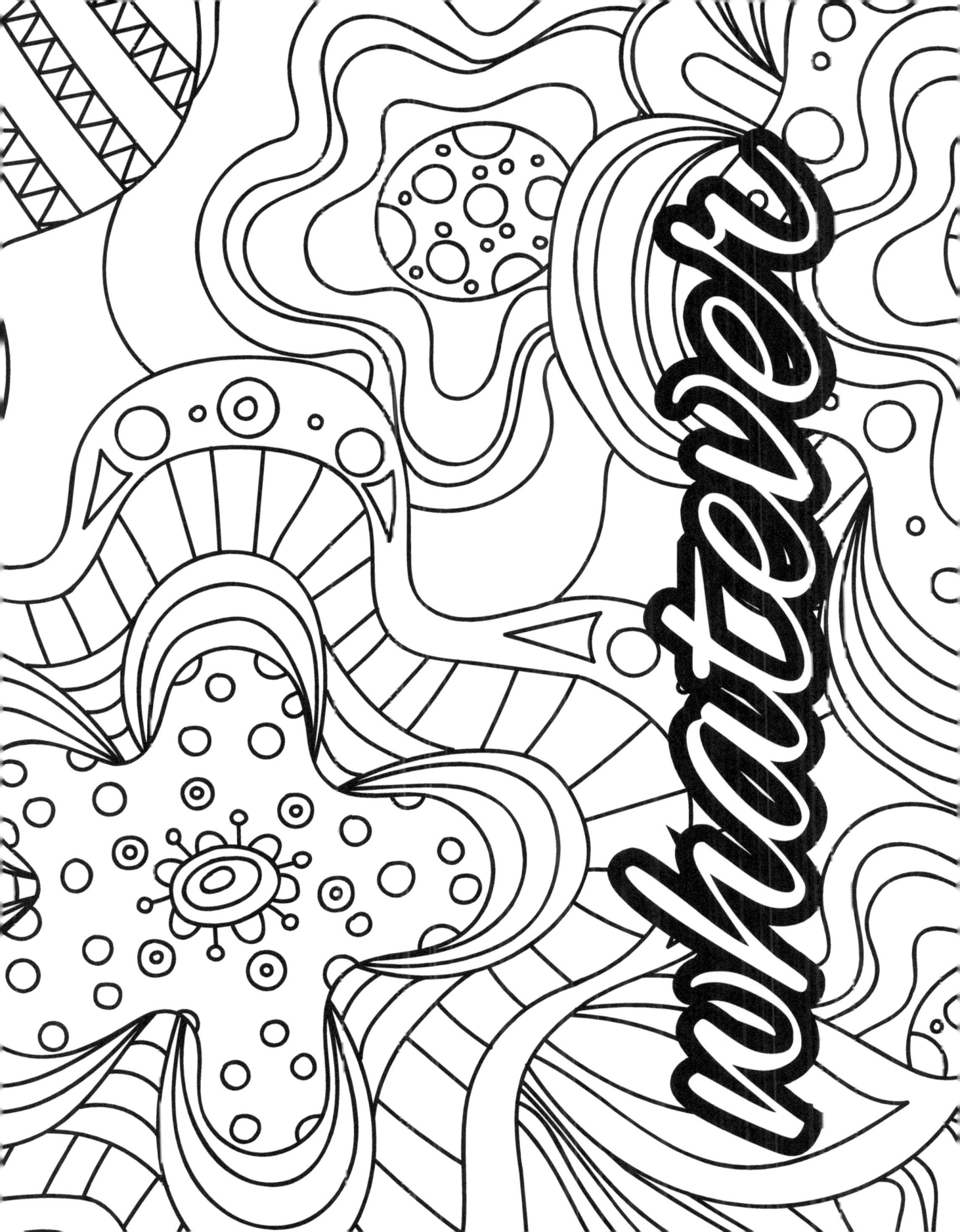

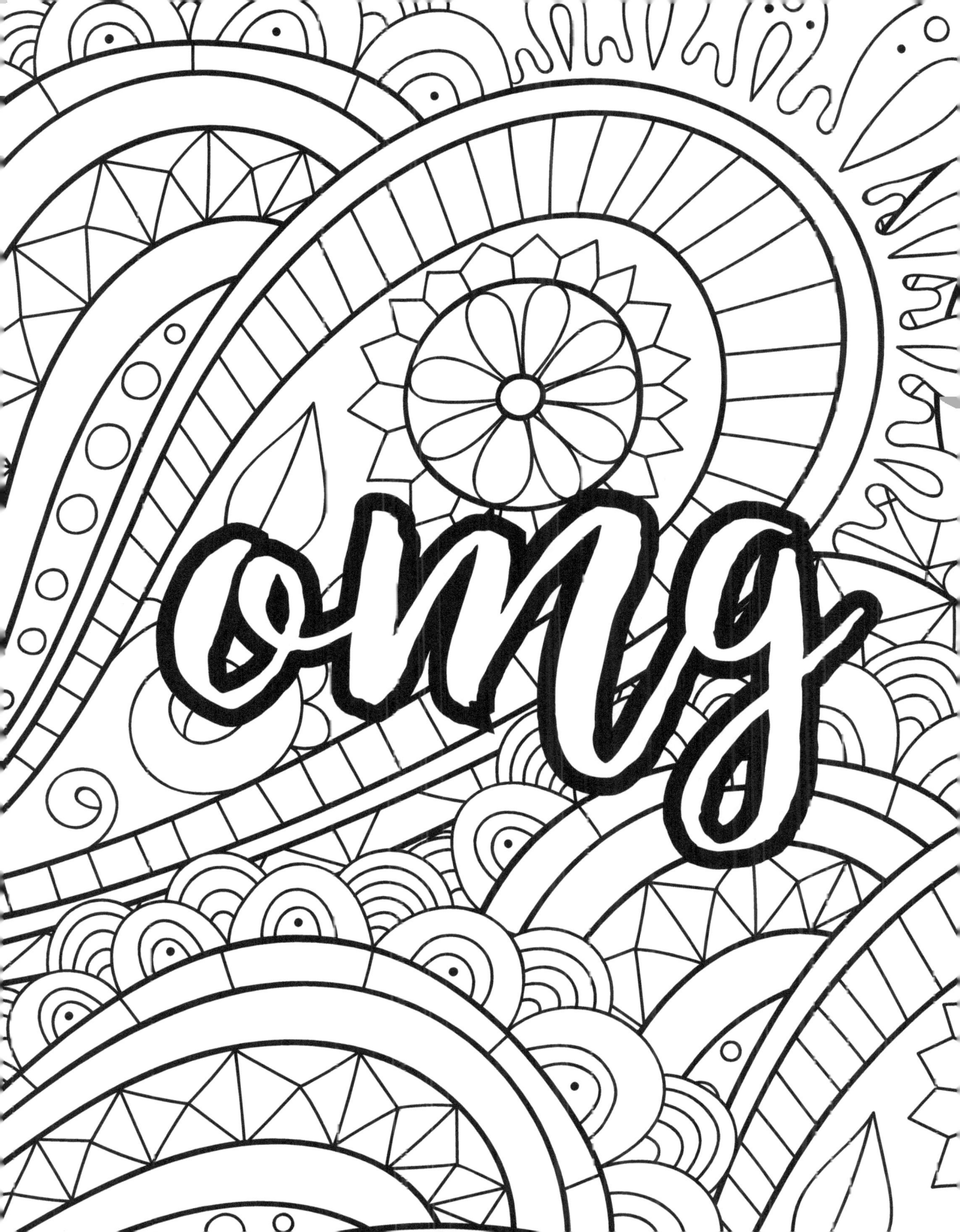

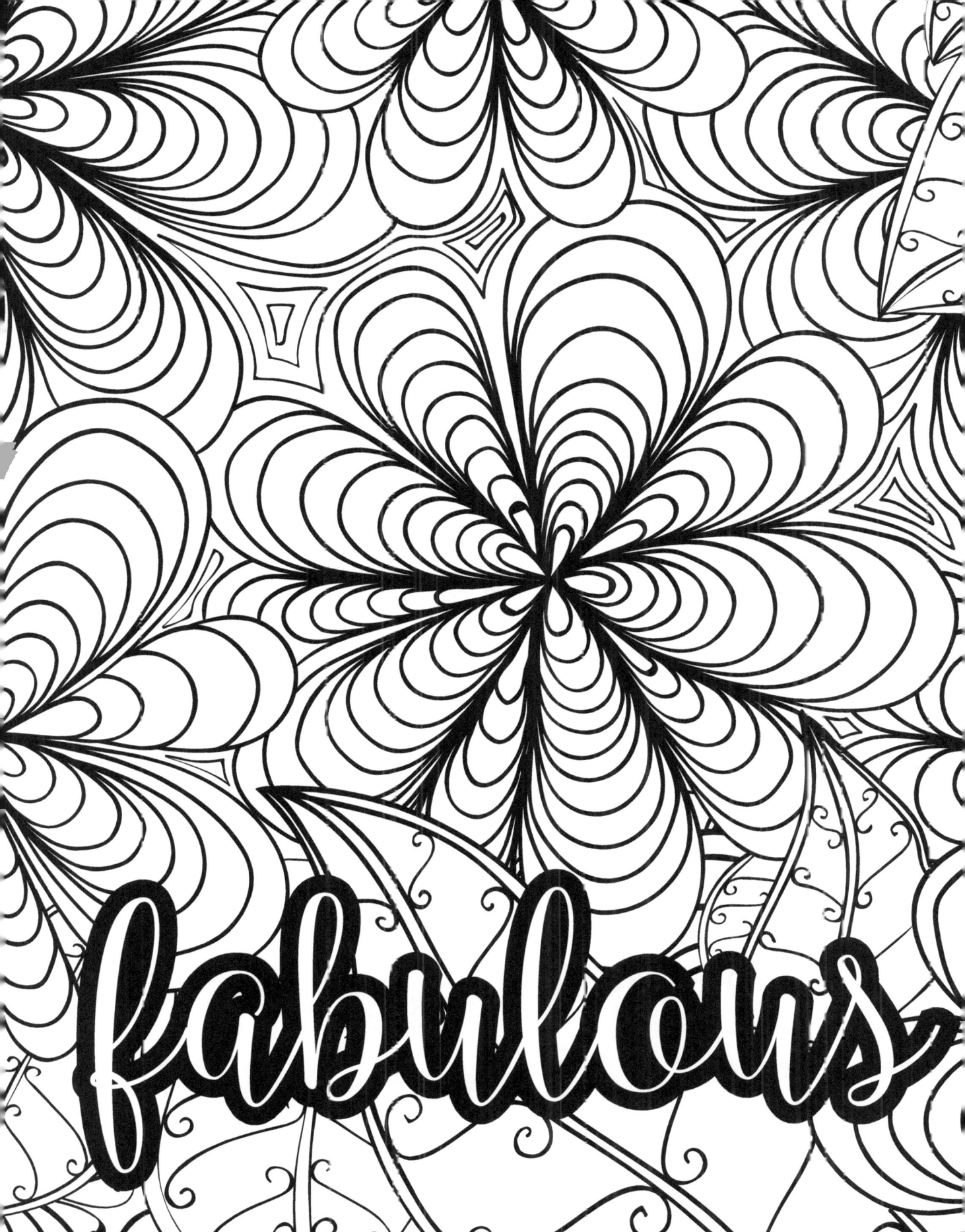

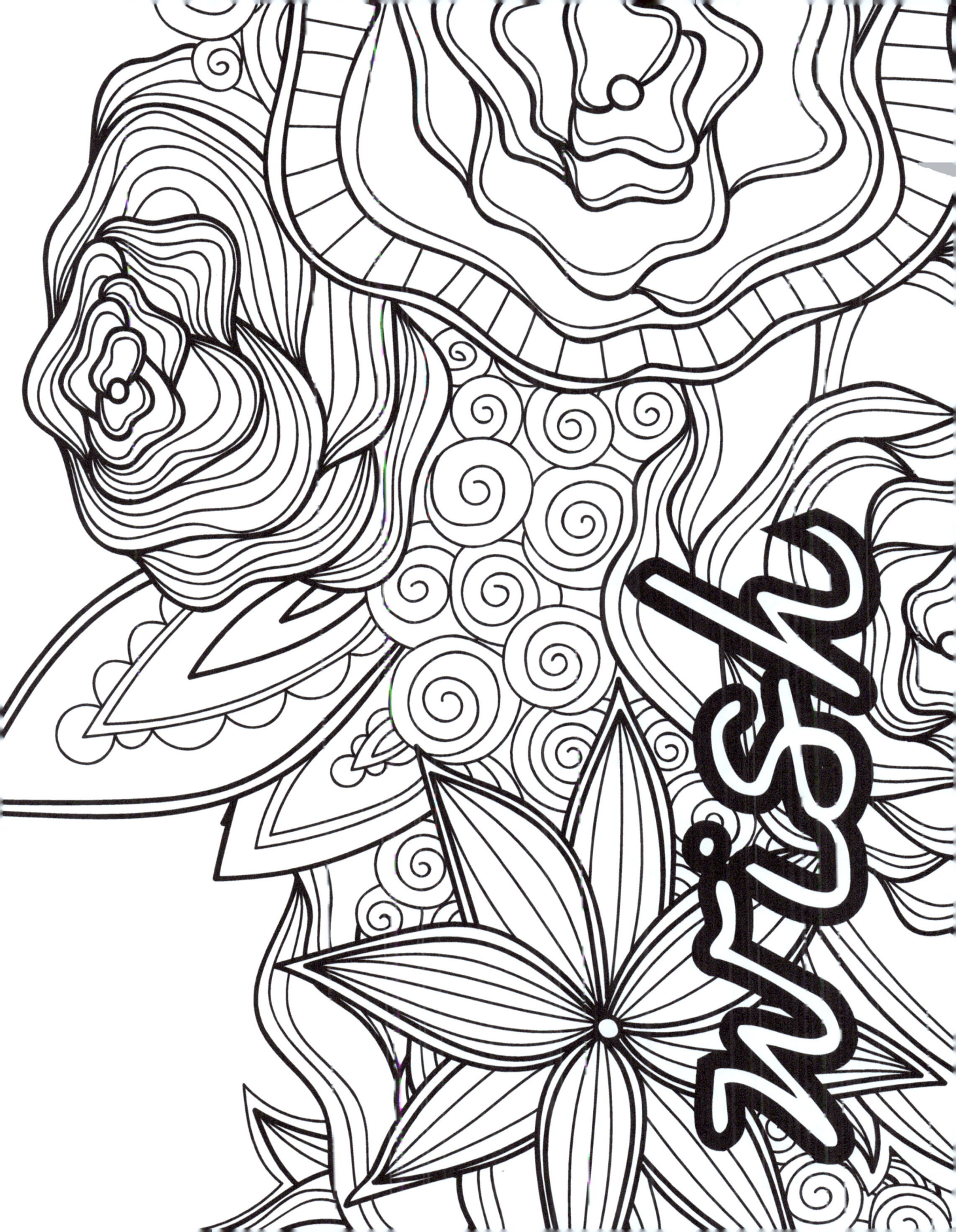

www.ingramcontent.com/pod-product-compliance
Lightning Source LLC
Chambersburg PA
CBHW080543190526
45169CB00007B/2618